Get Real!
Get Together!
Get Success!

By

Karen H. Hardin

Lexington, Kentucky

Get Real! Get Together! Get Success!

By Karen H. Hardin

Published by:
CoFriends, LLC
Post Office Box 23518
Lexington, Kentucky 40523-3518 U.S.A.
http://www.cofriendsllc.com

Although the author and publisher have made every effort to ensure the accuracy and completeness of information contained in this book, we assume no responsibility for errors, inaccuracies, omissions, or any inconsistency herein. Any slights of people, places, or organizations are unintentional.

ISBN: 978-0-9789777-0-2

Library of Congress Control Number: 2006909363

Printed in the United States of America.

Table of Contents

Acknowledgments and Dedication

I have been blessed to know many people who have contributed to and continue to teach me lessons about true success in life. Leaders, teachers, coworkers, friends, life-long companions, and especially my family have all been important in helping me understand my imperfections, yet how special it is to be loved anyway. By doing so, each of them has helped me to grow as both a leader and a person. If you fall in any one of the above categories—Thank You!

This book is dedicated to and in memory of a young woman who demonstrated in her brief 17 years what true life success really is. I count it a privilege and honor to have learned from her love, compassion, and even heartache for others. To Hannah, success was not about what you knew, what you achieved, what you owned, who you knew, or what people thought about you…it is about how YOU live. Thank you so much Hannah!

Dedicated,
in loving memory,
to
Hannah Meagan Landers

Foreword

I asked this young information technology manager to lead our company's Finance department and she enthusiastically responded that she wanted to help our organization in any way that she could. "However," she said, "I must confess that I know very little about accounting. In fact, I only occasionally balance my checkbook!" That was acceptable; because I didn't need an expert in Finance—I needed a leader.

It is not surprising to me that Karen Hardin has written a book on leadership—she has a passion for the subject. I know, because I had the pleasure of watching her grow and expand her own leadership skills from managing our Information Technology department to running the daily operations of our organization. Karen was a quality leader of Information Technology; however, the technical world was not where I saw her shine. She loved to identify the strengths in her employees and engage them in tasks that had to be done to make our organization successful. She recognized that she did not and could not excel in every job that had to be accomplished for our company and that to be successful herself, she needed to help others who were experts in their jobs to become leaders. Karen and I shared an aversion to complacency, recognized that work is only one element of an individual's life, that everyone can improve, and that every organization is uniquely identified by the collective efforts of its employees. She applied these principles to not only develop her own leadership effectiveness, but helped others become leaders also.

Having been in management for more than 40 years, I have come to appreciate the need for excellence in leadership. The pace of change requires teamwork to accomplish all of the work that must be accomplished and teamwork requires effective leaders. *Get Real! Get Together! Get Success!* brings together the skills, knowledge, and behaviors needed to help leaders improve, and provides tools they can pass onto the leaders of tomorrow.

Well done, Karen! "Keep up the fair work!" ☺

Roger Fries
CEO, Kentucky Employer's Mutual Insurance

Introduction

Having begun my career as a computer programmer, I was responsible each day for telling a box how to do exactly what I wanted done. With each instruction, the box responded, with no hesitation or criticism, but rather with obedience and compliance, regardless of how erroneous or ridiculous my instructions. Because I demonstrated my competence in making the box do what others needed it to do, I was promoted into a leadership position. Needless to say, the people I supervised did not respond as did the box when instructions were given! I quickly realized that many of the skills effective in completing technical tasks were of little use in effectively leading others.

I know that my inauguration in a position of authority is similar to how many "leaders" are born. Supervisors and managers have to suffer through trials and painful mistakes, trying to identify and then fit together the various pieces of the leadership effectiveness puzzle. Failures in putting the various pieces together have caused many supervisors and managers to simply stop their quest for the best of leadership skills and accept their existing skills, whatever they are. Because their leadership development has stalled, they cannot instruct or direct others to effective leadership either. Consequently, the individuals they promote to positions of authority must forge their own leadership development path. It becomes a troublesome and costly cycle.

I have been fortunate to work with various people who were effective leaders for their employees. My growth as an effective leader was simplified by the experiences they had in connecting all of the behavioral, organizational, and relational pieces of leadership together. Additionally, as an executive, I realized the need to develop leaders in a more focused and efficient way. I wanted to provide them with a picture of what an effective leader looks like and an approach they could follow to develop each individual's skills. Leaders not only need to fit together all the pieces of effective leadership for themselves, but also develop a consistent method for helping others become successful leaders. *Get Real! Get Together! Get Success!* describes an efficient path to leadership effectiveness and a formula to help all leaders stay on that path. I hope it encourages you to prepare yourselves and members of your organizations to respond in a unified and purposeful manner to the realities of a constantly changing world.

> *When we are in doubt and puzzle out the truth by our own exertions, we have gained something that will stay by us and will serve us again.*
>
> *C. C. Colton*

Section 1

Leadership Development Today

1 | A Puzzling Process

IF WE WERE GIVEN THE CHALLENGE OF COMPLETING A 1,000–piece jigsaw puzzle in 10 hours, many of us who enjoy working puzzles would say: "Bring it on!" Our enthusiastic reaction would be based on a couple of key assumptions:

- We would know what the resulting puzzle picture would look like,
- We would have all the pieces before we begin.

Personally, I have developed an approach to working with jigsaw puzzles that I always apply. After reviewing the box top to look at the finished puzzle, I work the edge pieces first and organize the inside pieces by color according to the picture, working them as I recognize their "fit." This strategy has always proved to be reliable and successful.

But what if the assumptions of the puzzle-working challenge are wrong? Would our reaction to it be the same? Suppose we were not shown the completed puzzle. Also, suppose that the puzzle pieces were only given to us 10 at a time, every 6 minutes. Although not impossible, the chances of success in working the puzzle would certainly be affected by these conditions. Our approach would be much less structured and more reactive, based on the pieces we received and when we received them. In fact, we might begin with one approach for our first 20 puzzle pieces, but determine that we need to change our approach with the next 10. Many of us who might have successfully completed the puzzle, if we had initially been provided all of the pieces, could find ourselves frustrated and confused with this new challenge.

This process is similar to the way many leaders must develop their leadership skills. The finalized picture of what effective leadership looks like is not provided, and the skills necessary to be effective are acquired on an "as-needed" basis. Often, leaders will spend years trying to identify and learn all of the elements of effective leadership, but regrettably may adopt behaviors that hamper or even prevent them from achieving their goals. These behaviors become additional constraints, even obstacles, in efforts to meet the challenge of a supervisory or managerial position.

Unfortunately, "effective leadership" is a concept and not something that can be photographed. The following picture does a fairly good job of illustrating my definition of an effective leader:

The picture shows a person with followers. They have reached the top of the mountain of success together. Everyone in the picture is celebrating this accomplishment. They wanted this outcome. They have arrived at this destination together and are sharing in the rewards of success. Although I will use the word "leader" in this book to represent the authoritative roles of individuals when other employees work under their supervision, it must be understood that there is a great distinction between demonstrating effective leadership and simply holding a management or supervisory position. One is a title and the other is a working reality. I very much appreciate and agree with the distinction between leadership and the other roles that individuals in supervisory functions play, as described by John

> *Real leadership is being the person others will gladly and confidently follow.*
>
> *John Maxwell*

C. Maxwell in his book, *Developing the Leader within You.* If we only show others how to do tasks as we do them, we are teaching. If we complete tasks through others, we are managing. Only by inspiring others to do the job better are we truly leading.

This book is about the latter, real leadership—having the skills and characteristics necessary to influence our employees and to inspire them to be their best. The key words here are "influence" and "inspire." Consider some of the many ways we can influence others: through power, control, manipulation, fear, encouragement, support, or motivation, to list a few. In fact, it is fascinating that each of these methods of influence can be associated with an effective historical leader. However, speaking as an employee, I prefer to work for someone who encourages and supports me rather than manipulates or scares me. Most employees share this desire. Throughout my career, I have found that leaders who use positive methods of influence have a more consistent and sustained impact on organizational success.

Therefore, our goal is to pursue leadership effectiveness by developing skills and characteristics that positively influence and unify others to meet our organization's goals. The following figure lists some important elements of leadership: "pieces," if you will, of the leadership puzzle.

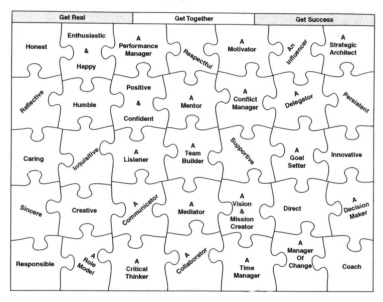

Many of these qualities will be mentioned within the context of developing our personal, relational, and organizational effectiveness: *Get Real! Get Together! Get Success!* The bottom-line is that effective leaders are those who work to develop their character (*Get Real!*); relationships (*Get Together!*); and skills (*Get Success!*) with equal attention and passion, and who inspire the same in their employees.

To cover each of these areas appropriately, this book has been organized into sections. This first section, "Leadership Development Today," discusses how leaders usually develop their skills and the pitfalls inherent in this approach. As we have already experienced in this chapter, knowing the elements of effective leadership and having an idea of what effective leadership is, are important first steps. However, I also believe that before we can attempt to do anything new, we must first know from where we start. Chapter 2 illustrates and discusses the approach most business leaders take to develop their leadership skills. Chapter 3 reviews the behavioral pitfalls of this development path. Among these pitfalls are traditions, habits, and routines that can become integrated into leadership that can make leaders less effective. These chapters help us understand where we are and how we got here.

2 | The Path Most Traveled

MOST PROMOTIONS FROM ENTRY-LEVEL TO SUPERVISORY positions are made to acknowledge that employees have demonstrated proficiency, quality, and dependability in completing tasks. Most employees enter their new positions with a boost of enthusiasm. They are energized by the fact that their employer has recognized and valued how they performed.

Because there are usually no guidelines provided to acquaint new supervisors with the responsibilities of their leadership role, it is natural for them to continue **focusing** on job tasks after their promotion. They do not realize the vast difference between the skills needed to accomplish tasks and the skills needed to lead others. Consequently, many leaders develop their leadership knowledge and behaviors through trial and error.

Because new leaders have already completed tasks effectively, it is natural for them to continue focusing on tasks after their promotion. They tend to assume their leadership roles only when situations within their areas of responsibility require it.

For example, a local engineering firm promoted a man into a leadership position just 3 weeks before the annual performance appraisals were to be completed. The company had no training in the review process and simply provided this new leader with the forms he was to use to evaluate his five employees. Because the previous leader of this group had left the company, the new leader had only the prior evaluation forms on which to base his assessment. Although he had demonstrated his organization and communication skills in his prior position, he had only been on the receiving end of goal-setting and performance management. Regardless, he was expected to complete the appraisal process. To do this, he compared how the members of his staff had performed against his own performance prior to his promotion; after all, that performance had been rewarded. Although he did his best, he did not feel he was prepared to perform this evaluative role adequately. He related his experience to me in this manner: "I had been to the doctor many times, but that does not mean I was equipped to practice medicine."

In my own case, my first leadership responsibility was to manage an employee with a terrible attendance record. In one breath, I was congratulated on my promotion and told to take immediate action addressing this employee issue. Unlike my engineering friend, I had never been on the receiving end of an attendance reprimand. Needless to say, I was ill-equipped to handle a performance issue of this magnitude. I wish I could adequately express my relief when the employee resigned before I had to act.

This "trial by fire" is too often how skills are developed in the quest to become effective leaders. In fact, most business leaders develop their skills in a cycle of focus that tends to look like this:

Business Leader Development Cycle

Although we will discuss each phase in more detail, let's quickly walk the path together. As stated earlier, the immediate tendency when employees assume a leadership role is to focus on the tasks being accomplished. They evaluate how these tasks are being done against how they did them in the past or would do them. As leadership knowledge increases, they begin to realize that the skill level of each employee has a great bearing on their ability to complete the tasks successfully. So, they change their focus from tasks to helping employees develop job-related skills.

Leaders begin to understand that with the proper skills, employees can successfully complete tasks. However, as each member of their staff begins to improve, they realize that the work cannot be disjointed and that all of the tasks really exist for a larger purpose. They must then ensure that the quality, timing, and interactions of staff members be unified to meet the purpose for which the group exists. This is typically called teamwork. They recognize the need to set quantifiable goals to unify staff efforts. Care is taken to ensure that the individual goals of each employee support team objectives. As employees achieve established goals, these leaders begin to wonder if the goals they are setting are the "right" goals. After all, their group is only one part of a bigger picture. How does the team's achievement of goals help the larger organization? Stated differently, what is the team's purpose in the organization? By focusing on the team's ultimate purpose, they begin to modify team goals to meet their perception of what the organization needs from their group. Yet, do they really know what the organization needs? What is it the organization is trying to accomplish, anyway? They realize that for the individual members of their team to be truly effective, each teammate must contribute to the organization's purpose and goals. Time is then spent revisiting team goals, employee skills, and the tasks being accomplished to ensure each contributes to the overall organizational goals. Figuratively, they have retraced their steps and are looking at everything from an organizational perspective. Through this process, they grow to be more effective leaders for their businesses. They move from a limited focus on the familiar to a broad focus on their organization's purpose.

This does not seem like such a difficult path. In fact, the progression of thinking is quite logical. But, if it is so easy, why do so few leaders approach their jobs with organizational insight? Frankly, I have found that many leaders get stuck before reaching that level of development. Let me illustrate this by looking at each stage more closely.

New leaders begin by evaluating the tasks being accomplished. They feel they need each member of their staff to complete these tasks to the standard they achieved in their prior role. Therefore, they spend their time teaching employees how they would do the job tasks, were they not the "leader."

I have known several leaders who began their supervisory role focused on tasks, and although they grew in management responsibility, they never left this stage of the cycle. One gentleman in particular epitomized the pattern of behavior common to task-focused leaders. He wanted all questions about how a task was to be accomplished directed to him. He told his employees that they could not mess up any of the tasks for which they were responsible beyond what he had the capability of fixing. And, when tasks of high visibility had to be completed in an area over which he had responsibility, he did them personally.

Additionally, he hated confronting employees about their performance. Instead, individuals who were not performing as he expected were given tasks he felt to be the least significant or most easily corrected. He gave individuals who completed the tasks far more work to do. Thus, he used his task skills to avoid or correct problems rather than to focus on the development of his employees. This resulted in a group of individuals who rarely improved and an overworked group who resented how things operated.

In contrast to this man, leaders who move to the next stage of the development cycle change their focus. They spend time evaluating the skills needed from their staff members to complete the job tasks. These leaders put their energies and efforts into developing the skills of their employees.

One manager who remained in this stage did a very good job of training her employees. She had no problems in dealing with performance issues if they were task-related. However, if the individuals of her group did not get along, she worked to get each of them back on task and out of each other's way. She never dealt with the group as a whole. Morale in her area went up and down like a roller coaster, based on how the individuals were coexisting.

Leaders who want to be effective recognize that although their staff work as individuals, the results of the group's collective

efforts are evaluated by the organization as a whole. Hence, the individuals in their groups need to
behave in a unified manner. Leaders
recognize their responsibility to
become team builders, goal setters,
and motivators. They must bring the
individuals in their groups together
to work as cohesive units. Goals for
their teams become very important,
as they are what unite the efforts of

the different individuals. As leaders improve goal-setting skills,
measures are put into place to help quantify team successes.
Most of the time, there is a noticeable change in the performance of their teams when they can be shown where they are
succeeding and where they need to improve. The individual
employees use their skills to work together to achieve the goals
the leaders establish for them.

Unfortunately, a leader who remains in this stage of the
cycle tends to develop teams that seem separated from the rest
of the organization. I have worked as a peer with such managers,
and can share from experience that these managers and their
team members made working to improve the organization
difficult. The groups were united in purpose and believed that
the way they did everything was the right way. They expected
other groups in the organization to support their efforts. Additionally, they could never be convinced that they should change
anything in their performance. When the organization needed
to change, this group was always a united barrier. To say it was
frustrating for the rest of us is an understatement!

Effective leaders move beyond focusing solely on the goals
of their areas of responsibility. The best leaders realize that their
teams can only be truly successful, if they are helping the organization achieve its goals. These leaders recognize the benefits of

vision and mission statements when used correctly to unite all their organization's teams. They understand their organization's structure, and they know what is important to the organization's success. They promote collaboration among staff and peers and they expand their strategic thinking and planning skills. Business leaders must develop this orga-

nizational view of their world to become truly effective. With this organizational view, leaders will re-evaluate the goals, skills, and tasks of their teams to ensure they align with their organization's purpose.

A major drawback of the current development path for business leaders is that it delays learning the link between tasks they knew so well as employees and the role those tasks play in supporting their organization's purpose. Consequently, this can cause us to develop behavioral patterns that may hamper our personal or relational effectiveness. Because new leaders try to learn as they go, they tend to follow existing organizational traditions simply because they do not understand their businesses well enough to question them. They may follow established routines simply because they do not know what changes would improve the services their group provides their organizations. Or, they may develop habits because they are not focusing any attention on how their behaviors impact their influence with and on others.

These factors (traditions, habits, and routines) affect how each of us behaves in our leadership roles. We must recognize that the behaviors associated with them can either benefit or hamper our leadership effectiveness. Therefore, we must learn to recognize habits, routines, and traditions, then continually discern their usefulness to our organizations and to ourselves.

Character building begins in our infancy,
and continues until death.

                                        Eleanor Roosevelt

3 | Traditions, Habits, and Routines

How human beings interact with other people is known as social behavior. Individuals who assume roles in leadership often do not focus much attention on how their actions are perceived by their coworkers. As discussed in the last chapter, we assume that because our performance was acceptable prior to our promotion, that our behaviors were acceptable as well. As we focus on trying to develop the technical skills of leadership, however, we must also pay attention to behaviors.

Traditions, habits, and routines share a common theme in human social behavior—the actions are repetitive. From a leadership standpoint, these behaviors are often associated with our "leadership style." But, how are these styles developed? Often our approach to new responsibilities is to duplicate what we have observed of leaders believed to be successful. Unfortunately, this mimicking process can cause us to accept traditions, habits, or routines that may hinder our leadership effectiveness.

Traditions are beliefs, customs, or knowledge handed down from one person to another. They become so much a part of us that we follow them as if they were law. As a non-business example of how traditions work, let me share with you the story of the "holiday ham." A family had a tradition of preparing a ham for the holidays, following a specific and secret recipe. On this particular occasion, it was the teenage daughter's turn to learn the special process of preparing the ham. She watched each step intently, asking her mother to explain everything. As her mother cut the ends off the ham, the daughter asked why the ends of the ham needed to be cut off. Her mother considered the question and realized that she did not have the answer. She did it that way because it was what her mother had done. She told her daughter that she did not know for sure, but that they would ask Grandma when she arrived.

When Grandma came through the door, her granddaughter greeted her with the question her mother could not answer: "Why did the ends of the ham need to be cut off?" Her grandmother explained that that was the way her mother had always done it; she needed to ask her great-grandmother when she arrived. When great-Grandma arrived, the daughter again posed her question: "Why do we cut the ends off the holiday ham?" Her great-grandmother smiled and answered: "I am not sure why your mother does it, but I did it because my baking pan wasn't big enough."

This simple story illustrates the danger of blindly following tradition. As a business example, consider the many organizational leaders committed to maintaining the established power structure within their company. Structure is certainly not a bad thing, and is necessary for organizing tasks and assigning work responsibilities. However, if the structure dictates who must make all the decisions, this tradition will adversely affect the organization's effectiveness. More specifically, if we believe that certain decisions and activities can only be completed by us because of our positions, then we are likely allowing traditions to influence our effectiveness as leaders. We should ask ourselves these types of questions:

- Do employees believe that "rank has its privileges" in the company?
- Are promotions based on years of service, or are they based on qualifications?
- Can decisions be questioned by subordinates?
- Do leaders consider employees to be "subordinates?"
- Do leaders "wear" their titles and depend on them for their power and authority over others?
- How are organizational changes made?
- Are they only made from the "top down?"

It is important to identify leadership processes of our organizations that seem to be based more on tradition than on effectiveness. We need to identify them, and then determine how they help or hinder our companies. Furthermore, if we have made these traditions part of our leadership style, they could also be hindering our personal effectiveness.

> *Traditions are the guideposts driven deep in our subconscious minds. The most powerful ones are those we can't even describe, aren't even aware of.*
>
> *Ellen Goodman*

Unlike the deep roots of traditions, habits are actions that have become associated with our character because we repetitively perform them; in this way, they are generally personal. In a positive sense, habits make our actions predictable for those with whom we work. Unfortunately, habits can also adversely affect how we are perceived by others if we are unable to change them when needed. They are comfortable to us, but may be irritating to others.

Again, let me start with an illustration of a habit with which most of us can identify. How many people do you meet who greet you with: "Hi! How are you?" How often do you greet others in this manner?

Are you sincerely interested in each person or is this a simple greeting for which you are expecting a predictable response:—"I'm fine."

How would you react if the person stopped and began telling you in graphic detail how they were?

The answers to these questions will help us determine if this is a habit, or if the greeting reflects our interest in other people's lives.

Consider the leader who is habitually late to work or to meetings. She has formed a habit of coming to work later because she works long hours. She also allows events in the day to determine her arrival time at meetings. These habits are neither good nor bad. In fact, the organization benefits positively from the additional hours this employee works. The decisions she makes while others wait in a meeting to which she is tardy may be critical to the company's success. Stated differently, promptness is not a crucial factor in evaluating the performance of this individual for the company.

The problem with this habit arises when promptness on the part of the leader's employees is important to meet organizational goals. Regardless of how often the leader communicates the need for promptness, her habit of being late will have the greater impact on the employees' behaviors. The result is a reduction in her effectiveness. So, although habits are often personal, we need to evaluate them in a larger context, because they can prevent us from exhibiting the behaviors we desire from our employees.

Routines are fixed actions that can be associated with either individuals or groups. Let me ask you a question that will quickly demonstrate a common routine. How do you tie your shoes? Because we were taught this as children, we can complete it successfully without even thinking about it. We have our routine, whether this entails making two loops and crossing them, or making one loop, wrapping the other string around it, and then pushing it under the loop. We were each shown how to complete this task and we practiced it until we could do it without thinking—routinely.

> *How use doth breed a habit in man!*
>
> *William Shakespeare*

"Unlike habits, which are established by repetition, or traditions, which are established by emotional commitment, routines are intellectual. They are developed because they are believed to represent the correct way to accomplish tasks. Because routines are uniform practices, most leaders establish them as expectations of all employees. Once instituted, leaders expect routines to be followed."

Like traditions and habits, routines can help or hinder organizational and leadership effectiveness. If the existence of a routine helps to ensure consistency in the behavior of the team members or organizational units, then its purpose is not only beneficial, it is necessary. However, routines that do not provide practical and recognizable benefits, or that do not obviously correlate to the mission of the organization, can lead to missed opportunities. Such routines paralyze our ability to change.

The Swiss watch-making industry provides an excellent, albeit troubling, example of this phenomenon. The Swiss dominated watch sales and profits from the late 1960s to 1980.

Their manufacturers had established the standard in designing, improving, and producing quality watches; all other watches were evaluated in relation to this standard. The routines they had developed during the manufacturing process ensured reliability in the watches and as a result, they grew to hold 80–90 percent of the global watch manufacturing profits.

Unfortunately, the routines the Swiss manufacturers established prevented them from seeing the future of watch making. Swiss watch manufacturing leaders were not only committed to the standards they had established, but the routines they had created as well. When one of their scientists presented a new electronic quartz watch design to them, the leaders refused to consider it. Consequently, Swiss dominance in the watch-making industry ended within a decade of this innovation.

The leaders of Swiss watch-making companies were committed to the routines of putting gears and springs together in a quality fashion. That commitment prevented them from being effective in their leadership roles. Simply establishing the routine did not hamper their performance; rather, it was that they did not continually assess how their routines affected their decision-making. We must ensure that we never dismiss an idea simply because it contradicts what we routinely, habitually, or traditionally have done.

In this section, we have considered how puzzling and inefficient the approach to leadership development is for many business leaders. In fact, the path followed has barriers and roadblocks that serve to deter progress toward effectiveness. The barriers and roadblocks are often traditions, habits, or routines we subconsciously integrate into our behaviors. They can blind us to areas of inefficiency and cause us to become complacent in our leadership activities.

Therefore, the next section provides a different approach to developing our leadership effectiveness; a leadership characteristic we can use to challenge traditions, habits and routines when they are encountered; and a formula for developing our personal, relational, and organizational effectiveness along the way. Although the new path and formula for developing leadership effectiveness are not complicated, they require us to be comfortable with change. Therefore, the section concludes by describing the steps necessary to change successfully.

> *Never again clutter your days or nights with so many menial and unimportant things that you have no time to accept a real challenge when it comes along.*
>
> *This applies to play as well as work. A day merely survived is no cause for celebration. You are not here to fritter away your precious hours when you have the ability to accomplish so much by making a slight change in your routine.*
>
> *Og Mandino*

Section 2

The Effective Path

4 | A Different Path

THE PATH MOST COMMONLY FOLLOWED BY BUSINESS LEADERS IS not the only approach to leadership development. Professional sports managers follow a different path. They begin thinking in organizational terms from the beginning of their careers. Actually, their approach to leadership has three qualities that distinguish it from that of most business leaders.

Sports Leader Development Cycle

HIRED AS MANAGER

START

The Organization's Goals

The Team's Purpose within the Organization

The Team's Goals

Tasks to be accomplished

Skills of staff who must accomplish the tasks

First, professional sports managers understand that their performance as players has little to do with their success or failure as team leaders. Most baseball Hall of Fame managers did not have illustrious careers as players and, clearly, did not establish leadership of their teams based on how they played the game. If they had, they would not have been acclaimed managers. For example, Hall of Fame manager Sparky Anderson of the Cincinnati Reds started his Major League career as second baseman for the Philadelphia Phillies and then never played another season in the big league. Though not recognized as an outstanding player, he was much admired as a leader.

Second, all professional sports managers know that the organizations for which they work want their teams to win. Their vision is to be the best in their sport. A professional football team wants to win the Super Bowl each season. National Hockey League professionals want to be the Stanley Cup champions. This is understood from the beginning of every player and manager's career. The manager commits to this vision the day he assumes leadership of the team.

Third, managers understand the requirements of each position defined for their sport. For example, basketball teams have guard, forward, and center positions. The responsibilities associated with each position require different player skills. The managers identify the skills they feel are required of each position. They learn the individual strengths of their players and put them in the positions that leverage their strengths. Additionally, they know that the players must play well, both individually and together, to win. A Major League manager realizes, for example, that no matter how well the pitchers perform in each game, if the team cannot score runs, its success will be limited.

In professional sports, then, the manager begins his leadership career with an understanding of the goal of the entire organization and the specific goal of his team. The manager must develop a complete understanding of the various tasks required of each position on his team and the skills needed to accomplish these tasks. He does not evaluate his players based on how he played the game. Instead, he learns the skills of his players and places them in the position for which they are best qualified.

Research has demonstrated that the higher the quality of leadership on a sports team, the better the results. Individual player success is better too. Two of the most important roles of sports leaders are

1. Determining how and where within the team to leverage the strengths of their players.
2. Determining the training needs and means of motivating individual players to improve their performance.

Research has concluded that when these are accomplished effectively by leaders in any field, it has a direct impact on the success of the organization.

For the most part, the business leader's path runs opposite to the sports leader's path. The only exception is that both business leaders and professional sports team managers must understand the tasks before they evaluate the skills of their team members. As was discussed, once effective business leaders recognize how everything must fit together to meet the organizational purpose, they change direction. Interestingly, they begin to follow the path of sports leaders. The diagram on the following page illustrates this more graphically.

Thus, both time and efficiency would be improved in business if supervisors and managers approached their roles in the same manner as sports leaders. We need to recognize that our responsibility is to connect the tasks, skills, and goals of our team to our organization's purpose.

Although changing our leadership development path will not prevent us from encountering traditions, habits, or routines, it will cause us to challenge them. We have to discern if our activities are necessary and if they support our organizations. Challenging traditions, routines, and habits requires us to consider changes or even to eliminate some behaviors. When we creatively consider alternatives intended to improve what is currently being done, we begin our quest for innovation.

> *Do not go where the path may lead,*
> *go instead where there is no path*
> *and leave a trail.*
>
> *Ralph Waldo Emerson*

5 | Innovation

ONE OF THE CHARACTERISTICS EFFECTIVE LEADERS USE TO continually challenge themselves and others is innovation. Innovation should not be confused with invention. Invention implies that something new has been created. To innovate means to make new or renew. Additionally, making new or renewing by definition means that what is being introduced has already been created. Therefore, innovation is not invention; it is what makes inventions useful to others. And to be effective, all leaders must be innovators.

Consider again the history of the Swiss watchmakers. They were the inventors of the electronic quartz watch, but the innovators were the Japanese companies who put it on the wrists of consumers. A little company by the name of Seiko not only became aware of the quartz design; their leaders also recognized that this technology would revolutionize the watch industry.

Similarly, Henry Ford is a person we view as an inventor although his contributions to industry were in his innovations. His name is associated with the automotive industry and many people feel he played a role in inventing the car. But, Ford said he never invented anything: He simply developed ways to innovate other people's inventions to produce a car that most people could afford. Ford challenged the industry tradition of making cars one at a time and changed not only the tradition; he changed all manufacturing.

These examples illustrate the benefits of innovation to leaders. Whether we are evaluating the goals of our organizations, the tasks being completed, our employees, or ourselves, we must be able to visualize changes that can improve effectiveness. If we cannot imagine how job tasks could be improved, or what new goals would help our employees' progress in their contributions to our organizations' purpose, tasks and behaviors are likely to remain the same. Striving to be innovators will help us think beyond what we know at this moment to visualize things as they could be. Innovation is an important tool in our pursuit of leadership effectiveness. As previously stated, developing effectiveness in our leadership requires us to focus on improving our character (*Get Real!*), relationships (*Get Together!*) and skills (*Get Success!*) simultaneously. An innovative method by which we can perfect our concurrent focus on these areas of leadership is a process I call the "Effectiveness Formula."

> *First say to yourself what you would be;*
> *and then do what you have to do.*
>
> **Epictetus**

6 | The Effectiveness Formula

THE EFFECTIVENESS FORMULA—GET REAL, GET TOGETHER, GET Success, characterizes a continual process of leadership, learning, and behavior modification. Whether we are a supervisor, manager or executive, we can use the focus of this formula to help us continually improve our leadership skills. More importantly, it defines the approach to leadership that we, as mentors, should provide to future leaders.

The first area of focus is to Get Real. Getting Real means we must

1. know our leadership strengths and weaknesses.
2. acknowledge our need for and dependence on others.
3. work continually to improve.

Only by being genuine with others can we build the relationships needed to achieve both our personal and organizational goals.

Because an organization's success is directly related to the success of its people, the second focus of effective leaders is Getting Together. Remember the research regarding the success of sports teams: Success is more likely when leaders play to their players' strengths. To achieve success, we must know the strengths and weaknesses of the people with whom we work.

The most effective way to develop this knowledge is to know each individual on a personal level. By knowing a person, we can establish personalized goals. Without such knowledge, we will tend to use our past performance as the measuring stick, to which we direct and coach them. This will limit their potential and our team's potential as well. Thus, relationships are an integral part of meeting our job responsibilities.

The last focus area is Get Success. Effective leaders set not only their own sights and energies on success, but also those of their team members. A simple definition of success is reaching the goal we want to achieve. For leaders to attain success effectively, they must

1. know what they are trying to achieve and why;
2. inspire their employees to strive for that goal;
3. organize tasks to ensure the goal is achieved; and
4. measure the value of the goal in terms of the organization.

Consequently, Getting Success requires that leaders understand the purpose and mission of their organization, how their team goals work to accomplish that mission, and the constraints (time and resources) under which goals are to be achieved. Additionally, an organizational perspective keeps leaders from focusing their attention solely on their team's performance.

To illustrate this, consider a football team's coaches and players. In football, a team is subdivided into several smaller units. The team has an offensive unit, defensive unit, and several special units. Although each group has goals for their unit, they recognize the ultimate goal is to be a winning team. Playing great defense is only part of the picture. Playing great offense is only part of the picture. Special teams are part of the picture, too. The big picture is that they have to win games together to be successful.

Similarly, Getting Real, Getting Together, Getting Success is not a sequential process for leaders. Instead, leaders must work on all of these elements all of the time. The Get Real,

Get Together, Get Success formula requires continual and simultaneous assessment of

- our skills and behaviors,
- the skills and behaviors of our team members,
- the outcomes required by the organization,
- and how those outcomes will be achieved.

As we identify opportunities to improve in these areas, change must occur for us to be able to seize them. John C. Maxwell said, "You can have change without improvement, but you cannot have improvement without change." Because improvement requires change, leadership effectiveness requires change. We have discussed changing the path or approach we have taken in developing our leadership skills. We have illustrated the need to develop skills in innovation that will help us challenge the status quo.

Now we have defined a formula that requires us to evaluate our character, relationships, and business skills and make changes wherever necessary to improve. Therefore, before we delve more deeply into the specifics of getting real, getting together, and getting success, let's ensure we share an understanding of the process, stages, and management requirements of change.

> *All things must change to something new,*
> *to something strange.*
>
> Henry Wadsworth Longfellow

7 | Effectiveness Requires Change

In 1973, Martin Cooper invented the cell phone. It weighed almost 2 pounds and cost about $1,000. Twenty years later, a friend of mine obtained a "bag phone." It weighed a little over 4 pounds and was packaged in a neat 11" × 6" × 4" bag. Today, my friend carries a 4 ½" × 2" × 1 ¼" cell phone in her purse that weighs slightly over 3 ounces. Her husband carries one on his belt that not only makes calls, but also receives e-mail, tracks appointments, takes photographs, accesses the Internet, and plays music or videos. They have obviously adapted to this change in telephone technology over the past 30+ years.

Now let me share with you how her mother adapted to this change. When her oldest daughter obtained the "bag phone," it was suggested that she get one as well. Her reaction was that she did not really enjoy talking on the phone and certainly did not wish to have one in her car. That remained her position on the subject until my friend's younger brother insisted their mother accept a phone about 5 years ago. He wanted to be able to get in touch with her, even when she was not at home. Although their mother accepted it, she kept it attached to the power adapter in her car and often forgot to turn it on when traveling.

Why was there such a difference in the reaction of my friend and her mother to the use of the cell phone? Your initial reaction may be that age caused the difference, but her dad embraced cell phone technology long before her mother, and he is older. The real answer lies in the process by which people come to change.

Although there are many theories about human change, for the purposes of this text, I will discuss one of the simplest. Kurt Lewin established a theory that has become a fundamental model in change management studies. He suggests that for any change to be successful, the participants must move through three separate stages.

The first stage is called "unfreezing." In this phase, a person not only begins to consider the need for a change, but also develops a sense of urgency to move forward with it. Once the person has committed to making the change, the second stage, "changing," occurs. During this time, the person decides what behaviors must change to meet the perceived need, and then works to change them. Once the new behaviors are moving, the person in the desired direction, "refreezing" must take place. This will make his or her new behaviors a consistent part of their existence.

The reactions to the cell phone varied between my friend and her mother because of the process they went through to recognize the need for change. When my friend's husband purchased the bag phone, she was five months pregnant with their first child. To ensure that she had a way to contact her husband at all times, she needed a cellular phone. Because the urgency was there, they committed to the new change rapidly. Once they possessed the phone, all of its personal and professional uses became apparent and they integrated the change into their lives. Today, not having her cell phone with her is like forgetting to wear her wedding ring—all day long she is aware that it is missing.

Her mother, on the other hand, did not feel the urgency or even the need for a cellular phone in 1993. She felt that her life was simple and someone in their family could always find her if she were needed. Without the feeling that a cellular phone was necessary in her life, change did not occur. Within the last year, however, she has begun keeping her cellular phone with her. What changed? Her grandchildren have cellular phones and with their parents all working, they may need to reach their grandmother for immediate assistance. This created her need for the phone and the urgency to change her behaviors.

Each member of this family traversed the stages of change to incorporate the use of cell phone technology into their lives. They simply did it for different reasons and at different times. Accordingly, the story demonstrates a key fact about change—it requires a personal decision to act. We must keep this fact in mind as we work to Get Real, Get Together, and Get Success. When we identify an element of personal effectiveness we need to change, we alone are required to act. However, this is not the case when trying to improve  our relational and organizational effectiveness. In those areas, change must be accomplished with others at the same time. Therefore, having a clear understanding of the steps involved in each phase of change is not only helpful: It is necessary.

Unfreeze:

1. Identify that a change needs to be made.
2. Pinpoint why the change is needed: What is the goal?
3. Clearly describe how things are currently.
4. Clearly define how things should be after the change is made.
5. Develop urgency in moving from where things are to where we need them.

Change:

1. Develop a specific plan of the steps required to move from where things are to where they need to be.
2. Define measures and benchmarks to mark progress toward the new desired state.
3. Execute the plan.

Refreeze:

1. Establish methods of ensuring new behaviors are being consistently used.
2. Consciously assess the behavior regularly to make certain the desired state is being maintained.
3. Determine if the goal of the change was achieved.
4. Repeat all steps as necessary.

With this common understanding of change, we can look specifically at what must be done to Get Real, Get Together, and Get Success!

> *Change your thoughts and you change your world.*
>
> *Norman Vincent Peale*

Section 3

Get Real!

8 | We Are Not Perfect

As WE BEGIN THIS SECTION, LET ME REMIND YOU OF OUR GOAL. We want to pursue leadership effectiveness by developing skills and characteristics that positively influence and unify others to meet our organizations' goals. We have committed ourselves to evaluating the tasks and skills of our employees from an organizational perspective. However, this only helps us approach our job responsibilities with the goals of our organization in mind. It does not help us to identify specific skills or characteristics we need to improve. That is the purpose of the effectiveness formula.

The first element of the formula requires us to identify and change things in ourselves that hamper our positive influence on others. In premanagement roles, we focused on the tasks we were assigned to complete. Although we may have been affected by the work of others, we were not responsible for it. We needed to get along with our coworkers, but the strength of our relationships with them generally did not affect our ability to accomplish our goals. Additionally, leaders evaluated our success on the goals we accomplished individually.

As leaders, focusing our attention on only tasks and goals will make our leadership impersonal and disengaged. Certainly, we will have relationships with our employees simply by

working with them. How-
ever, because our success is
greatly dependent on the
efforts of our staff, we need
to develop effectual relationships with them. Effectual
relationships are those char-
acterized by mutual respect,

open and honest communication, shared interest in success,
and a commitment to address behaviors, not personalities.
Notice the interconnection between our behaviors and our
ability to have potentially effective relationships with others.
The fact is, our behaviors are generally what sabotage our relational effectiveness. Therefore, if our behaviors do not promote
strength in our relationships with our coworkers, we need to
change them.

Getting real calls for us to continually assess our personal
behaviors toward others: the good, the bad, and yes, even the
ugly. Additionally, getting real must begin with an acceptance
that each of us has behaviors that we need to improve. It can
be difficult to face truths about our shortcomings—especially
when we need to be self-confident to do our jobs. But we
must be realistic, too. Regardless of the position we maintain,
we are not perfect. We have flaws that can make us less effective
in our jobs and in our relationships. If we are unwilling to
face the realities of our own shortcomings, we will likely be
ineffective in our attempts to help others improve in theirs.

The good news is that most of us readily admit that we are
not perfect. We know that there are things about ourselves that
can be improved. Although we may not have given it much
thought, we also know how we want others to perceive us as
their leaders. To demonstrate this, let's pick 10 positive traits
from the following list of characteristics that we would like
associated with our leadership behaviors.

ambitious	conceited	generous	resourceful
argumentative	conscientious	gullible	respectful
arrogant	cooperative	happy	rude
attentive	courageous	honest	sarcastic
autocratic	creative	humble	self-centered
boastful	demanding	imaginative	self-confident
bold	dependable	independent	self-controlled
bossy	determined	inventive	selfish
brave	disagreeable	loyal	sincere
bully	discreet	malicious	stubborn
calm	dishonest	moody	temperamental
caring	enthusiastic	obnoxious	trustworthy
cautious	fair	receptive	unfriendly
cheerful	friendly	reflective	wise

Essentially, we have now described the behaviors we believe would make us most effective in our leadership roles. Now the big question: Do our behaviors support the characteristics we have selected? We likely believe that for the most part, they do. However, our influence on others is not determined by how we view our behaviors; it is based on the perceptions others have of them. And many of us rarely seek to determine what those perceptions are. We must understand that to influence others, they must perceive our behaviors as consistent and predictable.

For example, one characteristic associated with effective leadership is honesty. Leadership literature supports that continually exhibiting honest behaviors fosters trust in an organization. Wonderful! Most of us probably feel a sense of confidence that we are honest and

trustworthy people. Unfortunately, it has been my experience that our employees often consider us as less trustworthy than we think. In fact, this difference in perception is often associated with behaviors we never suspect will affect impressions of our honesty.

Consider how such variations in opinions can arise. The leader of a local investment firm continually tells his employees of his belief in delegation and empowerment. In fact, whenever an employee faces a challenging decision and asks for the leader's help, he responds with, "Do whatever you believe is right." The employees make decisions and take the action steps they believe are correct. Yet, when there is a failure to realize the targeted results, the leader intervenes in the role of coach and asserts that he foresaw this outcome. He then proceeds to explain what should have occurred.

Regardless of how this leader feels that he is executing leadership fundamentals (delegation, empowerment, and coaching), his employees do not appreciate his leadership methods. In fact, they believe that the leader is either not being honest about his foresight or that his coaching should occur when they ask for his help. Because this occurs regularly, employees believe that the leader's claimed foresight is really nothing more than embellished 20/20 hindsight. Each incident of this sort causes them to further question his truthfulness.

We might be tempted to dismiss this example, believing that it illustrates behaviors that are not representative of most people. Unfortunately, this is much more the rule than the exception. Researchers believe that within a 10-minute conversation, more than 60 percent of people will lie at least once. Think about this number. If we engage in 10 discussions spanning just 10 minutes each, 6 will contain at least one lie. So, why do people who want to be honest do things that damage their trustworthiness? The reasons are varied, but most researchers agree that the person who lies wants to remain in control. The control allows them to avoid the punishment they believe may result from the truth. It may also ensure that they are well liked and perceived to be competent, as in the case of the investment leader. Lies are also told to keep from being hurt or to avoid hurting someone else. Regardless of the reason, a perception that a leader is untrustworthy will harm his or her overall effectiveness.

Remember, how we behave toward others determines the traits they associate with our characters. Honesty is only one of the positive traits we are likely to list as characteristics we aspire to have associated with our leadership. Furthermore, there are many other traits that we don't want mentioned with our

names. Look again at the list of characteristics in the table at the beginning of the chapter. Suppose in addition to being considered honest, we want to be considered attentive, respectful, calm, responsible, innovative, and receptive. Yet, we tend to interrupt or tune out others when they are talking; lose our temper when things don't go our way; never own up to our mistakes; conduct regular meetings that don't accomplish anything; and demand that others do what we tell them without questioning us. The chances of the desired characteristics being associated with our leadership are slim-to-none. In fact, the perceptions are likely that we are inattentive, disrespectful, temperamental, arrogant, wasteful, or autocratic. Understand that what we do in a repetitive manner determines how we are perceived by others. Additionally, if those behaviors prevent others from associating positive characteristics with our leadership, we need be aware of them and consider making a change.

The reality is that we are likely unaware of the behaviors that are most problematic in our relationships with others.

I have heard this referred to as the "bad-breath" syndrome. Although our mouth is no more than an inch or so below our nose, we don't know what our own breath smells like. However, those around us are all quite aware of it. Perceptions of our behaviors follow the same reality. We will be unable to identify what we need to unfreeze without discovering the opinions and insights of others.

Suppose we were to ask 10 people who work with us to select 5 traits from the previous list that they feel best describe us. Although the lists would vary in specific content, several characteristics would likely appear multiple times. What would be the most selected character trait? Would the adjectives selected to describe us be those we most want associated with our character? More importantly, how reliable will the feedback be? Will the people we ask be candid and honest with us?

Certainly, there are organizations that have developed and fostered open communication among their employees. If we are lucky enough to work for such organizations, we may be able to obtain candid feedback about how our character is perceived.

One of the instruments organizations of this type use to promote such communication is the 360° review. This performance review process provides employees with feedback from their supervisor, peers, and employees. To promote sincere and candid feedback, these reviews may

> *There are few nudities so objectionable as the naked truth.*
>
> *Agnes Repplier*

even be accomplished anonymously. In such cases, the person reviewed receives a synopsis of everyone's feedback without knowing who made what comments or ratings. The process is designed to provide every member of the organization honest feedback that can continually help us improve.

Regrettably, it is often difficult for those who care for or work with us to tell us we have "bad breath" in a direct and constructive manner. Even when we ask for and encourage input about our behaviors, people tend to feel that negative feedback causes conflict. And, conflict is something most people work to avoid. So, to obtain this type of input, our coworkers must feel that no conflict will arise from expressing their opinions.

In one organization, the leadership decided to institute the 360° review process. They believed that if properly controlled, the review's feedback would help all employees set more effective personal improvement goals. Because they did not have a culture truly conducive to open communication, they decided to preserve the anonymity of those who provided comments. They felt that by eliminating the fear of conflict, everyone could honestly express their views. To ensure this was accomplished, the procedures for the review were to be developed by Human Resources (HR) and tested by the leaders prior to asking all employees to participate. The plan called for each leader to evaluate all the others and provide their review forms to HR confidentially. HR would summarize the comments for each leader and provide the written feedback to each individual. The goal was to allow the leaders to experience the process and then provide their personal impressions of it. At that time, a determination would be made as to whether 360° reviews would be instituted for the entire company.

The method developed for completing the review was executed and controlled as planned by HR. Feedback was provided confidentially to only the leader for whom it had been summarized. The leaders met to provide their opinions of the process. All of the leaders thought they had received insights that could help them improve—except one.

Unfortunately, one executive did not like some of the comments made about his leadership. He shared several summarized comments that he resented with the group. Then, he informed the group that he must know who harbored those feelings about him. He called meetings, polled the employees involved, and told the managers that he had to understand why he had been criticized. It consumed hours of organizational time. Rather than viewing the comments in the context of learning and improving his effectiveness with others, he spent his energies trying to determine who said the things he did not like. Needless to say, the process was never implemented in the company. Word of the failure of the 360° process spread throughout the organization and perceptions employees held that open communication would result in conflict were reinforced.

I share this for two reasons. One is that if we are going to ask for the sincere perceptions others have of our character, we must be willing to accept and consider them. This is not suggesting that everything every-

> *When J let go of what J am,*
>
> *J become what J might be.*
>
> *Lao Jau*

one says needs to be acted upon, but we should never ask people for their opinions and then require them to justify those opinions to us. Appendix A provides an easy exercise by which we can obtain character-related feedback in a confidential manner. The instructions stipulate that no attempt will be made to identify the source of the information provided. Its purpose is simply to see if there exists a recurring opinion of our character that is inconsistent with how we want to be perceived. The bottom line is that if several people characterize us with a trait we do not like, we need to determine the cause of the perception. We are not perfect—it is likely that our behaviors need to change.

Secondly, trust takes time. Initially, we may have to obtain feedback regarding our personal effectiveness from sources other than our coworkers. Although, we can develop an environment and behave in a manner that encourages and supports open communication, the trust necessary for others to provide us the feedback we seek may not yet exist. Therefore, to ensure we acquire the feedback needed to help us Get Real, we can seek other sources for this information. For example, help may be obtained through a reputable educational environment. Many excellent leadership effectiveness and management classes can assist us in this area. Additionally, for those of us who have years of experience and, possibly, years of troublesome habits, traditions, and routines, personal coaching might provide us the assistance we need. Whether we seek this assistance in a classroom or one-on-one, our development toward personal effectiveness needs to begin with an objective assessment of our behaviors. Once we identify the behaviors that hinder our positive influence on others, we can commit to change and improvement.

9 | Influence, Not Popularity

As we set ourselves to the tasks of changing, we must keep one objective clear in our minds: We want to positively influence and unify others to meet our organizations' goals, not become popular. Although our character must support sound relationships, our goal is to influence others positively. For example, we need to be friendly toward others because it is a positive action, not as a method of trying to make others like us. Similarly, we should not be generous with others so that they will be generous with us in return. Manipulation versus influence can often be determined by who benefits from the outcome. Manipulation seeks to benefit the manipulator. Influence seeks to benefit everyone. All of the behaviors to which we subscribe should not only help us personally, but also be viewed positively by others. In the unfreezing stage of change, we determined which characteristics we wanted associated with our leadership and which ones we did not. Now we must establish a plan for personal change. The plan identifies the behavioral changes we want to make. It

An Influencer

explicitly lists actions we want to increase to promote positive perceptions of our character. It also pinpoints the actions we want to diminish that have been associated with negative perceptions of our character. Lastly, it must ascertain how we are going to hold ourselves accountable for executing the plan.

The plans for changing our behaviors are straightforward. For example, suppose we find out during the unfreezing stage that most people consider us temperamental. Thus, we want to change to behave in a calmer, more consistent, and self-controlled manner. With a sense of urgency to improve, we identify a confidant to help hold us accountable to these behaviors. Our accountability partner is a trusted peer, supervisor, or coach who, though discreet, will confront us whenever we act in a temperamental manner. Our plan is set—now it is all about our actions.

We must recognize that our plan is only a map. To take the trip successfully we are required to make the changes. Abigail Adams said, "Learning is not attained by chance, it must be sought for with ardor and attended to with diligence." We cannot allow the pursuit of our personal effectiveness to be left to chance. Change is difficult to make and even harder to sustain. Therefore, learning about human change can assist us in our diligent quest to improve.

First, we must recognize that our behaviors are often reflexive: We perceive, interpret, and react to events based on our experiences. Our senses provide information about what is occurring around us; our brain compares these signals with what we know and have come to expect. This process leads us to conclusions about the event. We base our reactions upon this quick, often subconscious thought progression.

As mentioned in the last chapter, according to research statistics, three out of five people will tell at least one lie in the course of a 10-minute conversation. Because I do not believe most people intentionally lie, I believe the untruths are spoken in a quick and reflexive manner. The individual has a perception of what his or her response needs to be, and asserts this, whether it is true or not. The desire to be perceived as likeable or competent is simply stronger than any perceived consequence of lying.

There are many opinions as to when it is appropriate to lie, but if our desire is to become sincere individuals, we must develop a plan for changing our reflexive responses. Although

our ultimate goal may be to change the perception that we are dishonest to a perception that we are honest, our change goal should be to stop and think about things we say before we say them. We need to consider our response in any situation carefully, and determine the response that is both truthful and wisely constructed. Thus, we must work to "think before we speak." In academic terms, this is referred to as critical thinking. Rather than allowing ourselves to react instinctively to questions, we commit to first examining the basis of our responses. We take time to consider the relevance and appropriateness of our thoughts in the current situation before we voice a reply. Refining our critical thinking will help us identify the role our reflexive responses play in our behaviors. We can then develop goals to help us restrain those reflexes.

A second factor to understand about change is that it is facilitated through our emotions. Researchers have confirmed that emotions play an extremely important role in initiating change. Therefore, it is important that change efforts be driven by a deeply emotional, even passionate, desire. The unfreezing stage of change requires us to have a sense of urgency to move from our current situation to something new. This urgency is born through our emotions. We tend to adapt our emotional attention to what we feel is most important.

For example, a man recognizes that he needs to put a new roof on his house. The existing roof has lasted over 20 years and he has begun to notice thinning spots on the shingles. He talks about the need to get a new roof with his spouse at least a dozen times over the course of 3 months, but he cannot seem to remember to contact a roofer. One night while they are sleeping a hard rain begins to fall. He is awakened by dripping water on his forehead. The roof is leaking. The following morning, he calls a roofer.

As this example demonstrates, we react to what we feel is most urgent. The need for maintenance on the roof did not generate the urgency necessary for the man to stop and call a roofer. However, once the roof started to leak, getting a roofer became his top priority. If we do not deeply feel the need to improve in the manner identified in the unfreezing stage, our behaviors will either remain static or change only briefly. To succeed in improving our personal effectiveness, our changes must be emotionally driven.

Lastly, we must understand a human's natural resistance to change. Change efforts are often abandoned when we fail to respond appropriately to the discomfort we naturally have with change. Because this resistance is a normal human response, understanding the common reasons for it can prevent us from giving up on our improvement efforts.

Rationalization is often an enemy of change efforts. We identify behaviors we wish to change, but then tell ourselves that those behaviors are exceptions to our "normal" actions. Because of this, we allow ourselves to believe that apart from these exceptions, our behaviors are consistent with our desired actions and therefore, change is not necessary. If we begin to think this way during the change process, we should give critical thought to why we identified these behaviors as needing attention during the unfreezing stage. Because the unfreezing process should have involved objective input from others, recognizing the behavior now as an exception is likely a sign of resistance.

Likewise, we may convince ourselves that our behavior was acceptable because it was a response to someone else; therefore, they are to blame. We reason that had it not been for their actions, we would never have responded as we did. Thus, our behavior was justified. Before deciding that our behaviors do not warrant attention, remember that we are responsible for our behaviors, regardless of others' actions. Hence, dismissing the need for change is likely an indicator of resistance.

Finally, we may feel overwhelmed by the attention we must give to our actions and reactions. These feelings can result in a sense of helplessness and we might once again rationalize that no one is perfect; others should accept us as we are, and we do not need the added stress of continually concentrating on personal change. But this source of resistance can, and should, fuel the fighting spirit within us. As we have agreed, no one is perfect and although we are trying to improve our personal effectiveness, we have not set our sights on perfection. We are simply taking responsibility for our own behaviors, and are assuming control of becoming a more

effective leader. The behavioral changes we want to make are targeted at self-improvement, and we are anything but helpless in our efforts. Like taking classes, exercising, meditating, eating healthy foods, or even reading a good book, this is something we are doing for ourselves. Feelings of helplessness or of being overwhelmed should be viewed as resistance. The truth is, that one thing in life over which we do have control is our own behavior.

Throughout the change process, we must recognize the roles that reflexes, emotions, and resistance play. We must utilize our knowledge of these impediments to avoid digression from our plan. Additionally, we must realize that as we change, our focus needs to remain concentrated on our objective, not on the reactions of others. Although each of us wants to be highly regarded individuals, our intent is to establish goals to improve our personal effectiveness and influence. We will never become effective leaders by striving to make everyone like us.

Regardless of the reactions we receive or the types of resistance we encounter, our efforts to improve should not be abandoned. Our leadership effectiveness is dependent on the qualities and behaviors we exhibit in our managerial or supervisory role. These behaviors can help us to become leaders that other people want to follow. Having had the courage to seek objective counsel, we have committed ourselves to new behaviors designed to improve our personal effectiveness. Now, we must dem-

> *People, like nails, lose their effectiveness when they lose direction and begin to bend.*
> *Walter Savage Landor*

onstrate our resolve and enthusiasm for making these behaviors consistent in everything we do. The success of attaining a goal that we have established for ourselves will provide us with more confidence in our ability to bring about needed changes in others. When our words and actions continually demonstrate the sincerity with which we embrace improving ourselves, we will find it easier to influence positive change in others.

10 | Unleashing Our Potential

A PLAN HAS BEEN DEVELOPED; OUR EFFORTS HAVE BEEN passionate and focused; our confidant has helped us stay the course. It would seem that the change process is complete. Not quite yet.

For the potential of our personal effectiveness to be unleashed, we must do two more things. First, we must refreeze our behaviors to the point that others recognize them as part of our character. Second, we must repeat the entire process.

What Lewin called refreezing is difficult. In fact, regardless of the area of effectiveness on which we are concentrating (personal, relational, or organizational) we will find constant pressure to change. This is actually a good thing, because it keeps us from becoming complacent and challenges our innovative spirit. However, it is essential to provide others with the time necessary to witness targeted behaviors in us, so they will associate them with our character. Consistency in our new behavior is required.

To illustrate this, let me provide you an example of a common derailment to change in the refreezing phase. Suppose a leader determined the need to improve her listening skills. She learned by working with an executive coach that she tended to be inattentive to others unless they were telling her what

she wanted or needed to
hear. So, she committed
to improving her listening
behaviors. She developed a
plan with her coach to
focus on looking the speaker
directly in the eye, using
gestures as evidence of her
attention, and summarizing

her understanding of the speaker's point of view before
responding. These behaviors are in fact appropriate and desir-
able in improving personal effectiveness.

However, just as perceptions of her behavior were changing, she was placed in charge of a new project that had to be
completed in a constricted timeframe. To finish the project on
schedule, she knew she must direct specific actions to each of
her staff members and prevent modifications to her plan.
Unfortunately, her employees had become accustomed to her
attentiveness when they wished to provide their input or voice
their concerns on any matter. On this project however, she felt
she simply did not have time to address their viewpoints if
the project were going to be completed on schedule. Her
executive coach drew her attention to occasions when she had
brushed off someone. However, she maintained that the
circumstances required her focus and associated abruptness.
She verbalized her commitment to improving her listening
skills, but the timing of the project simply was not conducive to
these new behaviors. Ultimately, she met the project objectives
as scheduled. However, the perception of her poor listening
skills intensified.

Although this leader modeled better listening skills prior
to the project, not maintaining those behaviors when the
pressure mounted actually fortified the long-standing perceptions others held regarding her character. Thus, changing our

behaviors for a short time, just to revert to our prior behaviors when things become difficult, can actually be more destructive than not making a change at all. This is where our commitment and resolve must be steadfast, regardless of what comes our way during the process.

Obviously, there were alternative behaviors that could have helped this leader improve her personal effectiveness while meeting her project responsibilities. They involve relational effectiveness that we will discuss in the next section. For example, she could have simply shared the stressors of the project with her team upfront. By directly communicating the time constraints and need to follow the established plan, she would have set the rules needed for the team to achieve success.

Unfortunately, the example illustrates how many leaders reject accountability for personal effectiveness during stressful situations. The executive coach did precisely what was needed— called attention to behaviors that were not supportive of the leader's personal effectiveness goal. Regrettably, the leader did not experience immediate or unfavorable consequences for ignoring her coach. Therefore, the accountability required from change became optional.

As leaders, we know that accountability plays an important role in employee performance management. Our employees have jobs they are responsible for doing, and it is our account of how they meet those responsibilities that measures their success. Additionally, if they fail to meet their commitments on a sustained basis, there are consequences. Research has shown that when people have to justify their performance to someone else, they perform at a much higher level than when their performance is not subject to evaluation.

Therefore, we must ensure that we are not only accountable for maintaining the new behaviors to which we have committed, but also that we have consequences if we quit. This is likely the most humbling part of the change process, because it requires us to obtain help and establish penalties in accounting for our behaviors.

Please, do not miss this point. Throughout the change process and beyond, there will be times when we will behave in a manner more consistent with our old ways than our new ones. Still, when our attention is drawn to the event, we must not use a method of resistance (exception, rationalization, helplessness) to justify our actions and put the goal on hold. When we realize our "slip," we need to

- determine where we failed;
- apologize to ourselves and, where appropriate, to others;
- then, recommit ourselves to the change effort.

This is where our personal growth occurs. Alexander Pope said, "A man should never be ashamed to own he has been wrong, which is but saying, that he is wiser today than he was yesterday." If we find that we are not able to maintain new behaviors, we must establish consequences that will provide us the extra incentive to succeed. Consider how the leader above might have responded to her coach if she had contractually committed to a financial penalty for each slip during the refreezing stage. Suppose she had agreed to give her coach $25 for each failure to demonstrate effective listening skills and $1,000 if she quit the process. Failing to sustain her new behaviors would have carried a personal consequence, giving her more incentive to stay the course. The fact is, we must take our commitment to personal effectiveness this seriously if we want to unleash our potential as leaders.

So, in the refreezing stage, we focus on making positive behaviors consistent in our response to others. Once the behaviors become a reliable part of our character, we must evaluate our personal effectiveness again. This is a lifelong process. It may sound exhausting—perhaps overwhelming—but put into perspective, it can be exhilarating. Consider this analogy. An overweight man is told by his doctor that to improve the quality of his life he must lose weight and commit to an exercise routine. Alas, one of the man's issues is his addiction to chocolate. He finds that every afternoon he must satisfy his chocolate craving by devouring at least two candy bars. With his doctor as his accountability partner, the man establishes a plan for change. He commits to a new diet; gives up his daily candy bars; and begins walking each day. Over time he loses the extra weight and finds himself in wonderful physical condition.

One day, the man misses lunch because of a meeting. He finds himself standing before the vending machine to buy something that will sustain him until dinner. Unfortunately, there it is—his favorite candy bar. He rationalizes that he has not eaten and one candy bar will not hurt him, so he purchases and enjoys it. As the days roll by, he finds that he is substituting lunch with candy bars more often. His work consumes more of his time and he exercises less and less. Over time, this man ends up right back where he started—overweight—with his doctor telling him things need to change.

You see, the man was not wrong to believe that one candy bar was okay. It was. The problem is that if we allow ourselves to slip back into our old behaviors too frequently, they will become our normal behaviors all over again. I have heard it said that a diet never works to maintain a healthy body weight; maintaining a healthy weight requires a commitment to a healthy lifestyle. Every day the elements of a good diet and exercise have to be part of our existence. Similarly, maintaining positive character requires a commitment to positive behaviors every day.

Before we leave the subject of personal effectiveness, let me emphasize one final, albeit important, observation. The challenge of modifying our personal behaviors to influence others should excite us. If we find that committing to the continual change associated with our leadership effectiveness makes us discontented, we should seriously evaluate whether leadership suits us. Everyone should seek personal improvements, but not everyone is impassioned to be a leader. For us to be truly effective 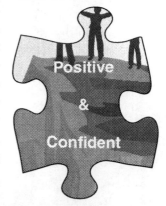 leaders, we must have a passion for developing positive behaviors needed to influence others. Also, we must acknowledge that not everyone is impassioned to be a leader of people. In fact, some people find interacting with others uncomfortable.

I have worked with individuals who found themselves in this position. They were promoted because of their excellence in completing technical tasks, but they never wanted to lead others. In one case, a young woman demonstrated knowledge and skills far surpassing all of her coworkers. Her leader, who was stuck in the first stage of the business development cycle, wanted to recognize and reward her for her performance for the organization. He did the only thing he knew to do to acknowledge her achievements—he promoted her into a leadership role.

This young woman had no desire to lead others. She loved working through the challenges her prior job presented; she even enjoyed showing others how to improve their skills. However, nothing about the responsibilities of leadership appealed to her. Although she committed her best effort to leading effectively, she hated the role. Because she lacked the skills and passion required in her new role, she almost lost her job. That would have been a terrible loss for the organization! This person, with the skills needed to help achieve organizational success, was almost let go because she did not have a passion to lead. Fortunately, she was able to work with Human Resources and other leaders of the organization to prevent that action. She was reassigned to a position that capitalized on her skills and passions. She has since re-established herself as an asset to the organization. More importantly, her passion and satisfaction with her work returned. She was happy with her job again.

Research not only encourages us to make changes that

support our deepest passions and make us happier people, it also suggests that by becoming happier people we will be more effective in engaging others. If we want our employees to be enthusiastic about their work, we must be enthusiastic about ours. If you have been promoted to a leadership role, but find the process outlined in this section disheartening, do not view it as failure. Recognizing where our passions are, in itself, is success. That is the goal of getting real!

We must also realize that personal effectiveness, relational effectiveness, and organizational effectiveness are all interrelated. One is difficult (if not impossible) to develop and sustain without the other two. If we are not intrigued by our behaviors' role in positively influencing others, it is unlikely that the work required to develop relational effectiveness will appeal to us. Furthermore, relational effectiveness is important for unifying employees to achieve organizational goals. If our talents and passions are in working on the tasks, not with the people, leadership is not a profession for us. Life is too short—we should pursue positions that provide us enrichment, satisfaction, and, if we are fortunate, happiness.

In this section, we have talked about improving our personal effectiveness. We must Get Real!—acknowledge that we are far from perfect and continually work to improve our personal behaviors. The following summarizes the process of improving our personal effectiveness:

- identify the characteristics we want associated with our leadership;
- determine where the perceptions of others vary from those traits;
- create a plan for change;
- acquire an accountability partner;
- institute the new behaviors by critically thinking about our actions and responses;
- ensure the behaviors become a consistent part of our interactions with others;
- repeat the steps to improve continually.

We discussed the role of accountability in our efforts. We also suggested the need to create consequences for ourselves if we find it difficult to sustain our efforts. Lastly, we discussed the importance of wanting and enjoying the process of self-improvement. Improving behaviors that increase our influence on others is never-ending.

The next section will describe another component of leadership effectiveness: relationships. The pace of change demands leaders use all of the resources available to them to succeed. One of the most important resources we have is our staff. Getting Together calls for us to open our eyes to the potential of this resource. Only by understanding the individuals, can we harness their potential to create a unified and focused team.

> *They always say time changes things, but you actually have to change them yourself.*
>
> *Andy Warhol*

Section 4

Get Together!

11 | People, People, People

IN THE LAST SECTION, WE DISCUSSED THE FOCUS WE NEED TO place on our personal effectiveness. But, our personal effectiveness as leaders is of little use without people. And, people are amazing! There are over six-and-a-half billion individuals in the world, and each is unique. These people belong to more than 880 ethnic groups, speak more than 6,900 languages, and may participate in one of 22 major religions. These statistics demonstrate a large part of what makes leadership a wonderful, challenging, and often frustrating experience. Indeed, with the global nature of business today, leaders must not only acknowledge the uniqueness of individuals, they must embrace their differences.

Typically, in the workplace, when we speak of having a diverse team, we are referring to a team made up of people of different genders, ethnicities, or nationalities. At times, we may even extend the definition of diversity in our group to include different skills or fields of expertise among our team members. We know research has shown that diverse teams exhibit more creativity and innovation than teams that are comprised of people of limited diversity. However, strictly speaking, diversity is a group of individuals with differences. So, in truth, any two people on our team will be diverse in some way. I have seen many teams with individuals of different genders, ethnicities, or vocations that do not provide the level of innovation needed by the team or the company. This typically occurs because these individuals, though diverse in many ways, solve problems in a similar manner, emphasize the same things as important, or work at the same level of detail. Although they appear to be a diverse team, the similarities in these qualities limit the team and may reduce the team's effectiveness. The real question of diversity that we need to ask ourselves is, "What are the various types of thought processes, opinions, or work styles that will provide our team with the skills, innovation, and critical thinking needed to ensure success?"

Let me be perfectly clear—diversity in characteristics such as gender, ethnicity, nationality, or job skills should always be considered important because limitations to views can exist without them. However, to be an effective leader we must go far beyond these characteristics and understand how our people evaluate problems, make decisions, think, and feel. We must know individuals on a much deeper level to understand what their presence on our teams provides.

Let me give you an example. Obviously, my husband and I do not share the same gender, but we have found through several leadership and personality instruments (e.g., Myers Briggs Type Indicator, Adversity Quotient, DiSC Management Strategy) that we are very similar in our thinking, values, and approach to tasks. Our lack of diversity in our thinking makes our marriage wonderful. However, I must admit that we do not elicit each other's creativity when a problem needs to be solved or a decision needs to be made. In fact, we tend to come up with the same solution. Unless we strongly disagree about the solution to a problem, we do not force ourselves to venture beyond what is comfortable. However, when we have to fight through our reasoning and objectives because we disagree, we most often reach a decision that is better than either individual's solution. Additionally, our sense of pride in the compromise adds enthusiasm as we undertake the task.

Coincidentally, the same phenomenon occurs with work teams. Too many similarities in the individuals' approaches to problem solving, deci- sion making, planning, etc., will constrain their creativ- ity and innovativeness. The characteristics of diversity discussed earlier are useful because the life experiences of people of different gen-

ders, ethnicities, nationalities, skills, etc., tend to broaden naturally the perspectives and ideas with which a problem is addressed. We must realize that though this is often true, it is only by getting to know individuals that we learn to accurately identify and appreciate their differences and similarities.

People are unique. We cannot successfully lead them unless we commit to developing the relational effectiveness needed to get to know how their backgrounds, opinions, views, values, etc., have an impact on the creativity and innovativeness of our team. After all, the differences we all have in these areas are what cause us to challenge one another to find common and often higher ground. A team needs:

- a person who thinks way outside of the box to be paired with a person who is adverse to risk;
- a person who has vision coupled with a person who is skilled at identifying every step of an effective plan;
- and a person who has a sense of what technology could accomplish if money were not an issue teamed with a person whose strength is attention to the bottom line.

These differences will cause team members to challenge one another and to work to find solutions that are far better than any one person could develop alone. This type of diversity helps both the team and the leader become more creative and effective.

As a final point, we need to recognize that as much as we need a diverse group of individuals on our team, we also need  the individuals to share some common ground. Work ethic, respectfulness, and dependability are a few characteristics that, if not shared, can cause conflict. Effective leaders do not simply assign people to their team. They choose those who possess qualities that provide diversity and innovation to the group, yet who share values that will bind the individuals together. Our leadership roles require us to identify the common ground our group must share to be successful. Then, we must never compromise those values when choosing team members. Yes, people are unique, but only when we take time to get to know each individual can we develop the relationships needed to understand their strengths and passions. Therefore, relationships are the heart of developing our relational effectiveness as leaders.

> *I've never met a person, I don't care what his condition, in whom I could not see possibilities. I don't care how much a man may consider himself a failure, I believe in him, for he can change the thing that is wrong in his life any time he is ready and prepared to do it. Whenever he develops the desire he can take away from his life the thing that is defeating it. The capacity for reformation and change lies within.*
>
> *Preston Bradley*

12 | Relationships

In the leadership development cycle of sports leaders, we found that one of their most important roles is matching the skills of the players to the requirements of each position. Thus, it makes sense that the more connected a sports leader is to the talents and passions of his players, the more likely he is to excel in assigning them to the most suitable position. This same matching of people to tasks is important in business. The more we understand the distinctive characteristics of our employees, the better we will perform this responsibility. So, how well do we know our coworkers? Can we answer the following questions about our employees and peers?

   a. How did they come to be employed at our organization?
   b. Did they attend college? Where? What was their major? Why?
   c. Where did they grow up?
   d. What do they like best about their job? What would they change about it?
   e. What do they enjoy doing when they are not at work?
   f. If money were no object, what would they want to do with their lives?
   g. What makes them happy?

h. Who are the most important people in their lives? Why?
i. Where do they live in proximity to their worksite?
j. What do they find most difficult about their jobs?
k. What do they hope to accomplish in their jobs?

Many leaders would say that most of the questions asked above are not pertinent to matching employees to tasks. In fact, they feel they only need to know what the job is and what the employee's resume says he or she can do. Other leaders would say they do not have time to develop close relationships with individuals with whom they work. The connection they share with their coworkers is simply that they work for the same organization. The fact is, both leaders and employees are being paid to do a job. So, should not the leaders be most concerned about getting job tasks done?

Actually, this thinking is far too narrow if we want to be effective leaders. Consider how individualistic the answers to the above questions are for each of our staff members. Each answer gives us insights into personal motives, passions, and interests where their jobs are concerned. Additionally, many things in life can adversely effect how our employees perform their jobs.

I asked a few leaders what factors outside of work would affect the way they perform their own jobs. Here are the most common responses:

- Personal illness
- Family illness
- Problems in a significant relationship
- Addictions
- Financial problems
- Tiredness or stress from being overextended (e.g., commitments to family, church, community, continuing education, family issues, etc.)
- Large personal decisions (e.g., buying or building a house, moving, purchasing a vehicle, etc.)

The leaders pointed out that although they do not want these types of personal concerns to influence how they perform their jobs, the truth is that they can, and do. If personal factors such as these are recognized by leaders as influences on their own performance, then we must acknowledge that they will also affect the performances of our employees. By understanding how life's circumstances and personal attitudes may affect employee performance, we will be better equipped to react proactively for the benefit of both our organization and our employees.

Unfortunately, many employees come to work, do their jobs, and collect their paychecks. They are not motivated or unified in their efforts to help make the business the best it can be. These employees would be the first to tell us that their jobs do not add to their lives' fulfillment—their jobs simply provide a source of income. This is unfortunate when we consider that most of us spend more waking hours each week with coworkers than we do with our family members. Consider:

- If those who work for us felt they were working with people who cared about their lives, problems, failures, and successes;
- if they were doing a job that challenged their skills and ignited passion within their souls;
- if they liked the time they spent at work because they knew they were doing something to help themselves and others succeed;
- if they looked forward to coming to work each day because they were valued; then work would not seem so much like work any more.

Research has shown that the happier people are with what they are doing and the environment in which they are doing it, the more productive and committed they are. In addition, companies that have been identified as some of the best places to work also tend to perform financially better than their competitors do.

As leaders, our relational effectiveness plays an important role in establishing this type of environment in the workplace. We are expected to motivate our employees. But, motivating others means nothing more than providing our employees with an urgency to act. Does this sound familiar? This is an essential part of unfreezing for change. Consider how personal and honest we have to be in evaluating ourselves and committing to personal action. The motivation comes from within us and it fuels the  emotion required for all behavioral changes and actions. If we do not know our employees on a personal level, how can we ever expect to help stimulate their desire to take action or change? Understanding what catalysts impassion our employees to perform compels us to dedicate time and effort to knowing them individually and personally. Much like the puzzle constraints imposed in chapter one, developing relationships in the workplace can be difficult. We have to make time to be concerned about what they think and feel, asking questions similar to those previously mentioned. We have to listen to each of them and genuinely care about their skills, interests, personal goals, and passions. By learning the unique qualities of each individual, we can commit our attention and energies to helping them become engaged and successful contributors to our organization. The bottom line is that as we practice being real with our coworkers, we must encourage them to Get Real with us. Relational effectiveness requires this, and this requires communication.

> *You've achieved success in your field when you don't know whether what you are doing is work or play.*
>
> *Warren Beatty*

13 | The Communication Connection

We have emphasized that attaining knowledge of our employees through our interactions with them is important in our efforts to Get Together. This implies that we:

1. seek to acquire information,
2. pay attention when that information is being presented to us,
3. and grasp the depth of emotion the person sharing with us has for the subject.

These are important elements in getting real and getting together: inquiring, listening, understanding, and sharing—i.e., communication.

Communication provides the connection between getting real, getting together, and getting success. Because it is essential to improving our leadership effectiveness, we must commit ourselves to improving our communication skills continually.

Finding the words to stress the importance of communication is difficult, but almost all leadership literature and training classes attempt it. Freeman Teague, Jr.'s, quote summarizes

why this is true: "Nothing is so simple that it cannot be misunderstood."
The unique combination that results
when any two people try to exchange
information makes this statement
undeniable. With some people, effective communication seems easy. With
others, it can be demanding. This is
why there are thousands of books
dedicated to helping us improve our
communication skills. They serve to
coach us on the elements of inquiring, listening, understanding, and sharing. We can use these resources to help us
continually improve our communication efforts. We just need to
Get Real!

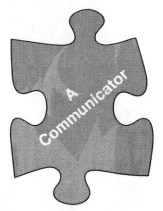

Over the years, I have identified several types of communication problems that hamper a leader's relational effectiveness.
Therefore, in this chapter we will review examples of business
communication that we need to avoid if we wish to develop
an open communication environment. I have called these
problems "shotgun communication," "misdirected communication," and "lack of communication." To quote the Berenstain
Bears children's book, *The Bike Lesson*, "This is what you
should not do. So let it be a lesson to you."

The first type of communication to avoid, shotgun communication, happens when leaders deliver a lecture or reprimand to all of their employees because of the actions of an
identifiable few. This communication shares the perspective of
the leader, but fails to use any other communication element.
Additionally, it avoids the one-on-one conflict associated
with directly addressing the person or persons at fault. I have
worked with many supervisors and managers who use this
type of communication when faced with sensitive or difficult

issues. Here are some examples of firing a communication
shotgun:

1. In an office where few employees take breaks, three women
   take every break provided together. They have developed
   an annoying habit of extending these breaks beyond the
   allotted 15-minute limit. Their behaviors aggravate their
   supervisor and coworkers. Unwilling to deal with the
   three women directly, the supervisor holds a meeting with
   his nine employees and informs them that the length of
   breaks taken is unacceptable.
2. An executive in a firm walks into her building with an
   employee she finds dressed inappropriately. Rather
   than discussing the issue with the employee personally,
   she has an email communiqué issued from her Human
   Resources department to all employees. It alerts them
   that "employees" have become lax in their compliance
   with the company's dress code and re-emphasizes the
   policy for everyone.
3. A department manager receives information from his
   computer administrator that a particular employee is spend-
   ing an unusually large amount of time surfing Internet sites.
   Additionally, the administrator knows that the employee's
   job does not require Internet research. The department
   manager therefore has Internet access removed from all
   11 of his employees.
4. A primary partner in a firm of more than 250 employees
   returns from an offsite meeting and witnesses an accounting clerk leaving the office for the day. The partner looks
   at her watch and realizes it is only 4:15 p.m. The next
   morning, every leader in the organization receives an email
   from her stating that work hours are from 8:00 a.m. to
   5:00 p.m., which they are to ensure is strictly enforced.

These are but a few examples of common responses from leaders who want to avoid conflict. The leaders use a shotgun blast to rid themselves of a perceived problem. Sadly, employees who do not deserve to be shot are wounded. The result of reprimanding employees for infractions they did not commit is always negative. Additionally, not addressing those who specifically committed the offense keeps them from recognizing or admitting that the reprimand was directed at them.

Relational effectiveness requires us to avoid shotgun communication. In the rare case where we must address an issue without knowing the specific group to whom it applies, we must establish a disclaimer apologizing to those uninvolved. Also, we need to provide the specifics of the issue to ensure those involved recognize easily their mistake. Let me stress that the problems that require this type of communication are rare. Therefore, do not use a shotgun; use a pistol, so you hit only what you are aiming at.

A second form, misdirected communication, usually occurs when leaders address issues without all of the facts. There are two ways to misdirect communication: a) criticize the wrong employees, or b) give credit to the wrong employees. Criticizing the wrong employees usually occurs in response to an issue or problem. For example, an organization's most profitable customer identified what they believed to be a billing error on their most recent invoice. The customer called the customer service executive at the company to determine the inconsistency in the billing and their records. The error infuriated the executive. He immediately summoned the organization's Human Resources (HR) manager. He reprimanded him for the hiring practices that would allow this type of sloppiness from their billing clerks and wanted the clerk who made the error removed from employment immediately. The HR manager was completely unprepared for this encounter. He knew nothing of the incident and could not readily recall the past performance of the clerk in question.

The HR manager investigated the error. What he discovered made this issue even more difficult for him. The clerk had failed to provide the customer with a 15 percent negotiated discount on the most recent billing. However, there was no documentation of this discount provided to the clerk. The HR manager consulted the customer's account manager to determine why the clerk had not been informed about the discount. The HR manager was told that the customer's sales executive had offered the discount at a recent meeting, but no paperwork had been completed regarding the discount.

The customer service executive's communication was therefore misdirected. The source of his frustration was with the actions of a peer, not with those of the clerk. Additionally, he chose to make his frustrations the problem of someone else—namely the HR manager. Had the executive taken the time to gather the facts about the billing error, he would have handled the issue much differently.

Equally as destructive as misdirected criticism, is misdirected praise. Consider the experience of a couple of associates in a marketing firm. They had worked 18 hours per day for 3 weeks to prepare a marketing campaign for a local brewery. Additionally, they never saw the partner on the account until the final days of review prior to meeting with the client. Once the campaign was completed, the marketing firm partners and these two associates met with the brewery executives for a review. The client was extremely pleased with the thorough work and creativity of the presentation. When the clients left, the managing partner of the marketing firm lavished praise on the partner in charge of the account. Unfortunately, the associates did not feel that the "nice job, team" comment made when the leaders were departing the conference room sufficiently acknowledged their hard work and dedication.

The praise from the managing partners in this case was misdirected. The managing partners probably had excellent reason to compliment the team, but the proper distribution of lavish praise was a problem. Again, the leaders had not researched the amount of time each team member spent on the preparation of the client's campaign. Relational effectiveness mandates that leaders allocate praise accurately. One other issue in this example is the lack of communication on the part of the account's partner, whose failure to direct the praise to his associates, who had earned it, was unacceptable.

Although the third type, lack of communication, can be less offensive, it can still affect our relational effectiveness. Consider the perceptions that can arise when communication is unintentionally lacking. A local construction company owner was aggravated with the discontent in his organization. It seemed that on a regular basis, his site leaders were unhappy and agitated and that their attitudes were affecting the contentment of his entire organization. However, the owner had always enjoyed the technical tasks of his business and did not like dealing with what he considered petty, touchy-feely issues. Even so, he knew he had to identify the source of the group's dissatisfaction to keep it from negatively affecting his company's future. He hired a consultant to determine the source of issues that irritated his staff and to provide him with a solution.

The first thing the consultant did was develop an understanding of the organization's history. The owner had established his company 15 years earlier and had always prided himself on having a happy and contented staff. Two years previously, he had taken himself out of fieldwork to concentrate on the management of his organization. He had identified six experienced construction supervisors to lead projects in the field. However, the restructuring of his company did not change his informal and often indifferent approach toward communication with his team members. In fact, he only communicated effectively with a couple of his leaders with whom he shared similar personal interests and hobbies.

Through interviews and confidential discussions, the consultant found out that four site leaders harbored feelings of mistrust, mistreatment, and resentment toward the owner. They believed he favored two leaders and always assigned them the most important and prestigious projects of the organization. Unfortunately, the increased communication he had with those leaders only served to confirm the perceptions of favoritism held by the others. Further inquiry determined that the owner had never communicated to his employees the skills he required when selecting the leader of important projects. Therefore, the leaders did not feel skills and abilities had anything to do with the owner's assignment process.

The consultant told the owner that the majority of his site leaders believed he "played favorites" when making project assignment decisions. He was stunned. He felt it was obvious that he needed to select his most qualified and responsible employees to meet the challenges of his organization's most important tasks. The two leaders he selected had more specific experience and qualifications than did the others. The thought that favoritism was involved in his assignments was ridiculous. The consultant asked him if he had ever communicated the qualifications he needed for different job types to all of his site leaders. The owner assumed they knew them. He was honestly oblivious to how the lack of communicating the skill requirements needed for each type of construction job was affecting his employees.

As was stated at the beginning of the chapter, the effectiveness of our communication will vary with each person with whom we interact. However, it can be guaranteed that errors of the type described in this chapter will interfere with our relational effectiveness. The last example illustrates the erosion of character that can occur if we do not share our expectations and perspectives with our coworkers. We will discuss the importance of identifying our group's purposes and goals as part of achieving success. For the purpose of communication, let me simply emphasize that open communication must begin with the leader. If we do not share with our employees, then it is unrealistic to believe they will share with us.

The first two examples illustrate a major communication issue for many leaders: conflict avoidance. As leaders, we will face a multitude of conflict situations. If we are to become relationally effective, managing conflict is a skill we must develop and communication is a key.

> *Only the curious will learn and only the resolute overcome the obstacles to learning.*
>
> *Eugene S. Wilson*

14 | Conflict— Communication's Dark Side?

WHEN PEOPLE ARE AROUND PEOPLE, EVENTUALLY A CONFLICT situation will arise. As leaders, we will find ourselves dealing with conflict with and between our staff members, coworkers, managers, and customers. Most people feel that conflict is the dark side of communication and is to be avoided. However, effective leaders understand that there is one critical fact about conflict that is fundamental: Conflict has the potential to be constructive as well as destructive. The difference is determined by how the conflict is handled. Therefore, effective leaders address all conflict situations quickly, directly, and decisively to bring about a constructive outcome for the organization. There are four ways of dealing with conflict: avoid it, work together to resolve it, get mediation assistance from a higher authority, or use power to dictate the resolution.

When leaders are not part of a conflict that arises between their employees, their first action step is to determine the gravity of the situation. If the issue will not jeopardize the ability of the team to achieve its goals, the individuals in conflict should be allowed to resolve the issue on their own. The participants may remain temporarily detached and frustrated, but as long as the communication between them is respectful and progressing, the leader should remain uninvolved.

For instance, a conflict arose between an insurance company's underwriter and the claims adjuster. The underwriter was responsible for managing one of the company's premier accounts and the adjuster was assigned to handle a sizeable property claim of that customer. The claims adjuster felt that the estimations she had made of the claim were reasonable and necessary. The underwriter knew that the estimated cost of the claim would affect his ability to maintain the pricing of the client's insurance coverage. The conflict began.

The claims adjuster informed her manager and the underwriter informed his. The two managers discussed the situation and agreed to have these two employees present them with a compromise solution. Although there were arguments and disagreements, these two employees continued to work together until they developed a solution they both supported. By working out the issue together, they had to seek an understanding of each other's perspective. They had to explore solutions that individually they would not have considered. Additionally, they came to appreciate each other's role with the customer. The leaders' only function in this process was to make sure their employees continued communicating.

Whenever we sense disappointment, disgruntlement, anger, stress, confusion, etc., among our staff members, it is our job as leaders to initiate communication. We focus first on listening to and grasping the perspectives of everyone involved. Then we evaluate what we have learned against our responsibility of ensuring that team goals are not adversely affected by the conflict situation. We can decide to ignore it and suggest others get beyond it. We can suggest the parties work through it on their own, or we can work with them as a mediator to reach a shared conclusion. Only when the conflict threatens to affect team goals adversely, should we intervene with the authority of our position.

When circumstances require intervention, we must provide decisive action. At such times, we do not seek the approval or agreement of the conflicting parties with our decision. We

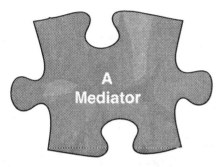

establish our actions based on what we believe will ultimately help us achieve our team and organizational goals. We listen, think critically, and then take the most appropriate action. We realize that the conflict can be resolved without agreement

on the solution. Though the persons in conflict may still harbor feelings of dissatisfaction about our decision, our communication with them should allow them to understand our course of action. Our leadership and sometimes our power must be used to move everyone beyond conflict situations to positive results for the team.

When we disagree with others and are a party to a conflict situation, our first response should be to determine the source of the dispute and what value it provides to our leadership efforts. Again, we must spend some time critically thinking through our position.

- Why are we bothered by the situation?
- Why do we feel our position is correct?
- Is our position supported by habits, routines, or traditions?

Ah, yes! We are back to getting real! If we determine that pursuing the dispute will not help our team attain its goals, we should avoid the conflict, apologize, when appropriate, and let it go.

If we determine that the issue has to be resolved, we need to work with the other individual to reach an agreement. Whether we are in conflict with our manager, a customer, a peer, or an employee, we must remain determined to work with them to a constructive outcome. Communication is the key. If the tension surrounding the subject makes one-on-one discussions unproductive, a mediator should be involved. This person's goal is to help us to clarify the differences in opinions that exist and to identify compromises we should consider. It is also important that this person have the positional authority necessary to ensure their suggestions are considered. If communication efforts fail, the mediator must have the authority necessary to resolve the matter.

However, in any conflict situation, our objective should be to resolve the matter through communication rather than power. As leaders, we must remember that there are always two sides when communication with others is involved. It is easy to get in a rush or lean on our positional authority in a manner that gives more credibility to the position we are communicating than to our interest in our coworker's position. For example, I once hired a competent, intelligent assistant who had an excellent background and strong academic credentials. Although I was 14 years her senior, we quickly discovered that we shared similar values and that our respect for each other was unquestionable. Unfortunately, we seemed to constantly argue and disagree on the details of projects we worked on together. Let me be clear, we always met our deadlines and the quality of our work was high, but the predictable conflict we had to work through to complete our tasks was aggravating. This was not how we wanted to model teamwork.

We agreed that the difference in our age had to play some role in our clashing perspectives. We decided to attend a class together on generational differences to see if we could determine exactly what that role was. It was amazing the enlightenment we obtained. I have the leadership approach of a Baby-Boomer. I believe that when a leader asks for something to be done, unless it is unlawful or immoral, the task should be accomplished with vigor. My assistant approaches work as an X-er. She needs to feel like she not only understands the outcome to be achieved, but is also part of developing the solution.

Although I felt I had listened to her point of view, I had to admit that I wanted her to accept what I said needed to be done, and then put her heart into doing it. After all, I was telling her how to reach the desired goal based on my experience. But, she could not engage completely in any project or process until she developed a personal connection with it. Although she did not have the authority needed to alter my project approach, she did have an environment of open communication through which she could vent her frustrations. When she did, I could not understand it and conflict arose. The class helped us understand the source of the conflict. Once each of us understood the other's perspective, we worked much more effectively with each other. We became one of the strongest work teams in the organization.

As leaders, we must accept the responsibility of managing conflict situations. We must expend the time and energy necessary to understand every person's point of view. We recognize that when communication is difficult, listening is usually the skill most deficient. Therefore, we work that much harder to acquire and understand the perspectives of everyone involved. Resolving conflicts with individuals requires work and persistence. To be effective, we must always look for the most constructive outcome possible for our teams and organizations and establish that resolution as our goal.

In the last several chapters, we have emphasized the need to expend continual effort in building our relational effectiveness with each of our unique employees. We acknowledged that our leadership communications (from the uncomplicated to the difficult) need to promote unity and openness within our group. We began with ourselves. Are we trustworthy? Are we good listeners? Are we caring? Get Real! If our characters do not support the trust, interest, and confidence required for open communication, getting together will be difficult. Then, we stressed the importance of communication to relational effectiveness. It cannot be understated. It is fundamental. Let me emphasize again that our goal in establishing open communication is not to promote our popularity. It is to make sure we understand our employees' passions, goals, and any life circumstances that might affect their performance. Each day our relational efforts need to keep us connected with our employees. However, our relational effectiveness must extend beyond connecting each employee to ourselves. Unless we are also able to connect their efforts, the unity that fuels success will not be recognized. Therefore, relational effectiveness also requires us to create a team.

Intimate relationships cannot substitute for a life plan.
But to have any meaning or viability at all,
a life plan must include intimate relationships.
                                                    Harriet Lerner

---

15 | Building a Team

WHILE GETTING REAL WITH AND WORKING TO KNOW EACH OF our employees may help us maximize individual strengths, it is also vital that employees form relationships with one another and bond into a team. It is the leader's responsibility to draw unique individuals together into a cohesive unit or team. The word "team" has been defined in a variety of ways. Certainly, a team implies that two or more individuals are working together toward a shared objective. Consider:

- A doubles team in tennis is made up of two people who are trying to win a tennis match.
- A basketball team has five players on the floor trying to make more baskets than they allow their opponents.
- A baseball team has nine players trying to score more runs than their opponents do.
- A football team has 11 players on defense trying to keep the opponent's offense from scoring, while their own 11-player offense works to score.

The objective of an athletic team is easy to define based on the sport's particular purpose and rules. In other words, a person does not join a baseball team with a desire to score touchdowns. To be more precise, members of a team wish to use their talents in a collective manner to win the game, whatever that game may be.

Teamwork in business follows a similar scheme. People are assembled to work together to achieve the purpose of the organization. However, this is a much easier statement to make than to accomplish. In sports, success is defined by whether games are won or lost, but success for a business team is often not easily articulated. It is difficult to verbalize with clarity the importance of each task and the quantifiable value it adds to an organization's goals. Challenging as it may be, it is our role as leaders to provide clear purposes for our teams. Continuing the sports analogy, they need to know how to play the game ("processes," "tasks," "skills"), the game rules ("expectations"), the positions ("roles"), and what constitutes a win ("success").

Much like a coach on the first day of practice, we need to establish expectations about how our team is to interact and perform together. At a minimum, we need to develop fundamental shared values and a conflict management process to which our team members will be held accountable. The most effective way to accomplish this is through the development of written team-operating principles. The forms in Appendix B can be used as an outline for drafting this type of document. It  has two parts. Part I is completed by each member of the team, including the leader. It shares information about the individual and his or her view of what is important to successful team interaction. Once completed, each member receives a copy of the leader and his or her teammates' input. Then Part II is completed by the group. It summarizes what the entire team agrees is important to their success.

As leaders, it is important that we set the example of getting real with our employees by completing Part I thoroughly.

- What skills do we offer that add value to our team?
- What motivates us?
- What gets on our nerves?
- What behaviors do we feel are important in the working interactions with each other?
- How should conflict situations be resolved?

We need to pay particular attention to the section on "pet peeves." "Pet peeves" are behaviors, events, or situations that consistently irritate us. We are generally aware of them and do not understand why they do not irritate others. As leaders, we have an obligation to identify all of the expectations we have of our team members, including behaviors that we know frustrate us. This is not often stressed in leadership training, but it is very important, because when we are annoyed, it will be evident to those who work with us. Additionally, if our organizations are accepting of behaviors that annoy us, our "pet peeves" can cause problems. The best way to illustrate this is with an actual example.

A manager has a known "pet peeve." She has always been annoyed when individuals arrive late to work. However, a year ago, her organization committed to flexibility in work schedules. An emphasis is now placed on getting the job done, not what time an employee arrives or departs the premises. Certainly, her annoyance with tardiness has not ceased simply because her company philosophy no longer agrees with it. She simply does not feel she can address this employee behavior as a performance issue just because it frustrates her. Unfortunately, she vents her extreme annoyance with employees who come to work late by identifying insignificant issues that allow her to reprimand them. Everyone knows that this manager has a tardiness "pet peeve," and she damages her credibility each time she projects her frustrations for employees' late arrival onto other subjects.

Many leaders would say that if the behavior, event, or situation is supported by the company, the manager should not react negatively toward it. I agree. Unfortunately, "pet peeves" are extremely frustrating for individuals and are often very difficult to suppress. They are even more difficult to change. As leaders, the best way for us to address them is to Get Real. We acknowledge them with our team and ask them for assistance in overcoming those that are contrary to our organization's philosophy. Communicating our "pet peeves" with our employees will keep them from being caught off guard when our frustrations over them flare. Although they are no more important to share than our motivations, behavioral ground rules, or expectations for managing conflict, they are often overlooked. To improve communication of our expectations, they need to be shared.

We discussed the importance of managing conflict in the last chapter. It is especially important in leading a team of diverse individuals. To ensure our team members understand how conflict situations are to be handled, we should make sure the process to be followed is defined explicitly. The following is an example of a conflict management policy that describes my desired escalation process:

Team members will try to resolve conflicts privately before seeking assistance from others. Matters of conflict will not be discussed with other employees unless leadership assistance is needed. If assistance is sought, it must be addressed with the team leader or Human Resources. Involving coworkers uninvolved in the conflict situation is unacceptable. Team members may be directed to choose whether they prefer to talk directly to the offending party or simply avoid the conflict by ignoring the offense. If the conflict remains following a private discussion, both parties should seek the mediation assistance of their leader(s). The inability to resolve the issue through mediation will result in the leader(s) establishing the solution. Occasionally, the leader(s) may establish the action that will be taken on the issue outside of this escalation process. This will occur when the leader(s) believes it is in the best interest of the project, team, or organization.

Communicating this information in a direct and open manner is one example of how expectations need to be shared with our team members. Whether we are disclosing our "pet peeves," conveying performance measures, or connecting the importance of tasks to organizational goals, we need to remind ourselves that communication provides the connection between getting real, getting together, and getting success. We should endeavor to hold employees accountable for only actions or activities about which we have shared clear expectations. It may seem unnecessary to talk about what language is appropriate, what attire is acceptable, what Internet sites or emails are fitting, or how illegal activities outside of the workplace would be addressed. But we must remember: People are unique. We should ensure that what is, and is not acceptable in the workplace is not left to personal opinion or belief. Consistency is valued in leadership and is vital in creating a cohesive team. Emphasize organizational policies and procedures, and put additional team expectations in writing.

The process of developing this document should be the beginning of many team-building activities. Taking time out to plan, evaluate performance, and have fun with one another provides the best opportunity to Get Real and Get Together. Unfortunately, many leaders do not acknowledge the importance of casual, fun staff interaction. However, it is unreasonable to believe that our staff can find characteristics in one another that can unify them as a team, if they are never provided opportunities to spend time together away from their job responsibilities.

Effective leaders not only recognize this as a critical element of team building, but they also make sure that time and events specific to this purpose are provided for staff. Team-building activities are utilized during staff meetings. Offsite workshops that focus on teamwork are attended together. These sessions teach employees about topics such as effective communication, brainstorming, project planning, problem solving, and conflict management. Research has demonstrated that teams who learn together are far more productive and creative than those who are never given that opportunity.

Additionally, effective leaders work to unify their employees by providing relaxing, fun time together. They take time out every once in a while to play during work hours. Taking half a workday to go bowling, play laser tag, or watch a movie can be time well spent for showing appreciation and fueling team morale. Equally fulfilling, is to engage the team in community projects such as working in a shelter, visiting a nursing home, or walking together for a worthwhile cause. Such activities are very important to team performance, so please do not make the mistake many leaders make and schedule these activities during employee off-work hours or at their expense.

Another small, but often-overlooked attribute of effective leadership is celebrating with our teams. Many leaders have no problem calling a meeting that involves thousands of dollars of employee time to discuss miscues, errors, or less than favorable outcomes. These meetings may be very productive and necessary, but when employees are only brought together to discuss what was less than satisfactory, team morale can suffer.

As leaders, we must also take time to acknowledge team accomplishments. Saying "thank you" can be done in ways that require little time or money, but yield priceless results.

Lastly, to be relationally effective, we need to personalize our team's unity by remembering birthdays, recognizing life events like marriages and births, and encouraging group support in times of personal difficulty or loss. By demonstrating consistent attention to the lives and circumstances of team members and by keeping the team involved with one another in both personal and professional ways, we can demonstrate that the individuals are more important than any work issue that may arise. We have heard many times that we must  address behaviors and never belittle an individual. Developing our relational effectiveness means going beyond this. We need to communicate the importance of each individual's role in the team's success. We must learn how to mentor others and share the wisdom of our successes as well as failures.

Thus far, we have established the need to evaluate all aspects of our jobs from our organizations' point of view. We commit to improving ourselves and strengthening our relationships with others. However, leadership effectiveness requires these efforts to yield positive results for our organizations. The responsibility of making our team the best it can be belongs not just to us, but also to every member of our team. Thus, the final element of the effectiveness formula focuses on bringing getting real and getting together in sync to achieve success for our organizations, our employees, and ourselves.

> *The quality of an organization can never exceed the quality of the minds that make it up.*
>
> *Harold R. McAlindon*

Section 5

Get Success!

16 | Are We Coaches or Captains?

Success is achieving goals we have established for ourselves. To this point, we have discussed several types of goals. We establish personal goals to improve our personal effectiveness. We also set goals to develop positive relationships with our coworkers. As we achieve goals in each of these areas, we will experience personal satisfaction and success. However, we want to become effective leaders, and that requires us to integrate our personal goals and relational influences with the goals of our organizations. This integration is accomplished following the effective leadership path. We develop an understanding of our organization's purpose and our team goals; then, we must unify our team members' skills to achieve them.

As leaders, we can participate in one of two roles with our team. Continuing the sports analogy, we can be either coaches or team captains. We either direct our team's activities like coaches (from the sidelines), or work as team members (or team captains) to achieve group goals. In this chapter, we will discuss these two roles and give support for why our being "coaches" is most important to our organizational effectiveness.

Coaches establish the expectations, exercises, drills, and plays that their teams will follow during daily practice sessions. They assess their team members' skills, offer instructions for improvement, and alter plays to maximize the strengths of their team members and improve performance. Effective coaches organize activities to get the most productivity possible from each practice. Additionally, they formulate game plans based on the progress they observe. The coach

determines the position each team member will play and when each player will play during the game. During a competition, the coach watches from the sidelines, shouting encouragement and directions.

Team captains receive instructions from their coach, just like all other team members. They work with their coach to make each practice session worthwhile and with their teammates to execute the coach's strategy. The team captains also give direction to their teammates and offer encouragement. However, they are part of the team. They are players. Their performance, like the rest of the team, is evaluated by the coach. They simply have the added responsibility of directing the activities of fellow players during the game.

Similar to sports coaches, business leaders set the sequence of the daily activities of team members through established policies, procedures, job descriptions, and workflows. They assess their team members' skills, offer instructions for improvement, and alter procedures to maximize the strengths of their employees and improve performance of their daily activities. Effective leaders organize these activities to get the most productivity possible in a day's work.

Similar to captains on sports teams, project leaders in business receive instructions from their leaders (the coaches). They acquire clarification of project expectations, guide project activities, and work with their teammates to meet project goals.

They have project tasks to accomplish and deadlines to meet. Additionally, their performance, just like that of their fellow team members, is evaluated by their leader.

Sports teams need to win games to establish themselves as the best. Business projects are identified to improve results and help the organization be "the best." In sports, game strategies are planned. In business, project strategies are planned. These plans are expected to draw each organization closer to its purpose. In both sports and business, preparation, planning, and execution by each member of the team are critical to success.

The leadership roles for sports managers on "game day" are better defined and controlled than they are in business "projects." In sports, the rules of the game define the distinction between roles of coaches and captains. The rules prevent coaches from going onto the playing fields. Captains are not only on the playing field; they are expected to direct and participate in the game. If a coach ignores the rules, the team is penalized. If captains do not work as hard as their teammates, it diminishes the team's chance of winning.

In contrast, business leaders often fail to define clearly their role for their teams. They can function as coaches or as team captains, and often oscillate back and forth between the roles. One minute they are helping with tasks; the next, they are telling others to do them. They say they are going to work with the team to develop project plans, yet commit to project completion dates without their teams' input. This blurring of roles can affect their personal leadership development, depress team morale, and ultimately affect the progress of their teams toward established goals.

We cannot be effective for our organizations unless we exemplify strong leadership for our team. That requires us to clearly establish our role on our teams and stick with it. If we are going to be coaches during practice, we should remain coaches during the game. When projects are required to achieve team goals, we need to assign project team members, appoint project leaders, and share the desired objectives with our teams. At that point, we need to commit to our role of coaches and step back to the sidelines.

This is difficult because we have a stake in the success of every team project. Consequently, we may feel the need to be active participants to help teams complete the tasks. We attend team meetings and ask to review the details of their work. These activities can interfere with creative planning and the implementation process. When this occurs, we have placed ourselves in the game and slipped from being coaches to captains.

To be effective, we must take care to limit our involvement in developing and monitoring project activities. Playing the role of both coach and captain hinders staff and team development. In fact, it prevents us from fulfilling one defining characteristic of effective leadership: developing future leaders. This cannot be accomplished unless project leaders are allowed to lead their teams and, at times, fail. Randy K. Milholland said, "We all have a few failures under our belt. It's what makes us ready for the successes." Effective leaders use their knowledge and experience to allow their project leaders and teams to fail in circumstances that will help them grow, but not preclude them from achieving  their goals. This requires critical thought to be given to every suggestion or directive before it is communicated. Although they want to provide their teams with the benefits of their experience, effective leaders recognize that what they say carries positional authority. The fact is, when leaders speak, their words carry greater authority than that of their project leaders and often more authority than the entire team.

For example, a colleague of mine was promoted to an executive position within his organization. His background was in engineering, yet his promotion positioned him as the leader of the organization's financial and administrative functions. He walked into a meeting of his financial staff just to say good morning. His team was in the middle of a procedural discussion and quickly debriefed him. As a trained problem solver, he processed what he was told quickly and made a suggestion for staff consideration. He wished them a good day and left the meeting. Several weeks later, he was approached by one of the finance department's best accountants. The accountant stated that a problem existed with the directive this leader had given. Naturally, he was concerned and asked the employee for the specifics of the directions. What he discovered shocked him. The suggestion he had made in the staff meeting was not considered as a suggestion at all. It was considered the solution. More than a solution, it was accepted as the course the staff was to follow. Although he never intended it to be so, his offer of assistance in the meeting weeks before had been viewed as direction. He quickly got the leaders of the finance group together, apologized for the misunderstanding, and walked away with a valuable lesson—leadership positions carry authority.

We must take care not to offer suggestions unless that input will help the team better understand their objective or learn from our experiences. We need to realize that whenever our teams feel we intervene in a project, they will stop working together to develop solutions and meet deadlines. Instead, they will rely on us to provide them with instruction and direction. In fact, they will wait for it. The benefits of the team structure fade away. In effect, as the coach, we have walked onto the playing field, taken over, and the players do nothing unless we direct them to do so. We simply must not allow this to occur.

Research has demonstrated the importance of team empowerment in improving project outcomes. Empowerment means that while playing the game, team members are allowed to work together to achieve their goals, drawing on their various talents and experiences. The team establishes the plan, divides the tasks, makes decisions, and accomplishes the tasks together. As coaches, we must be a resource of support and encouragement if we want our employees to unify and meet the challenge before them.

On the rare occasion when we feel we must get into the game as captains, we have several points of communication that must be made to the project team. The first point is why we feel we must join the team. The team needs to understand the circumstances that require us to get involved. The reason should express the organizational benefit of our joining the team's efforts. The second point of communication needed is our intent to share the responsibilities and tasks of the team. When we decide to get into the game, we must make it clear that we are to be considered one of the players. Third, we need to communicate our expectation that every team member remain involved, united, and productive in the project. We let them know that they are encouraged to challenge us as fellow teammates. Last, we ask them to provide us feedback if they view our participation as controlling or feel they have little influence on the course of the project. They must understand that the project cannot lose the advantages of teamwork. All of this communication must be made directly and confidently.

I believe one reason leaders struggle to maintain the coaches' role on team projects is that the initial expectations of the projects are vague. The link between the tasks that must be accomplished and their importance to the organization's purpose cannot be articulated. To be effective, leaders need to understand the organizational system in which they work and be able to communicate clearly how every project supports and improves it.

If business leaders fail to remain coaches because project expectations are vague, then our opportunity to improve our organizational effectiveness lies in improving our goal-setting and performance-management skills. These skills are necessary to establish, monitor, and improve our teams' contribution to our organizations. By committing ourselves to the effective leadership cycle, we ensure that we maintain a consistent view of our responsibilities from the organizational perspective. To be outstanding coaches for our teams, we must be able to establish concise performance targets and get the best performance possible from every individual. It is on this foundation that we develop our organizational effectiveness. Therefore, in the next chapter, we will delve deeper into the organizational systems of business and discuss the tools we can use to help us Get Success.

> *An empowered organization is one in which individuals have the knowledge, skill, desire, and opportunity to personally succeed in a way that leads to collective organizational success.*
>
> *Stephen R. Covey*

17 | And the Organization

BEFORE WE MOVE DEEPER INTO THE ORGANIZATIONAL ASPECTS of effective leadership, let's summarize what we have covered thus far. To develop our leadership effectiveness in the most efficient manner, we need to approach our responsibilities from an organizational perspective. Additionally, we must focus on three areas of development simultaneously: personal effectiveness (Get Real), relational effectiveness (Get Together), and organizational effectiveness (Get Success). To Get Real, we must understand that our behaviors and attitudes greatly affect our leadership effectiveness. Thus, to have personal effectiveness means that we work continually to improve and change characteristics about ourselves which diminish our ability to influence others positively. To Get Together, we acknowledge that every person is unique. With that recognition, we sincerely seek to know the goals, skills, and interests of each of the people with whom we work. The relationships we form will help us match the tasks to be accomplished with the person most equipped to complete them. It will also assist us in selecting our staff members and in uniting them into a cohesive team. The focus on our relationships with others can never be taken for granted or ignored.

To begin this section, we discussed how leaders participate on
their teams. They can lead and
direct the group or they can participate as a member of the group,
but should never do both. To
be organizationally effective, our
teams have to know our role and
be able to anticipate and count on our behaviors in that role.
Additionally, because empowerment is significant to our teams'
success, we should commit ourselves to leading the team as
coaches, whenever possible.

The next requirement for our teams is to develop an
understanding of our organization, the marketplace in which
it competes, and the challenges it faces. Most organizations
communicate this purpose through vision statements, mission
statements, and strategic plans. The vision and mission statements articulate how each company will meet consumer
product or service needs. The strategic plan is used to compare
the organization's performance to the vision and mission
statements. Through the comparison, goals are established
for the business that, when accomplished, will help the organization improve. Although not all organizations have them,
these declarations are considered fundamental to business
leadership. The written vision, mission, and strategic plans
are the tools by which an organization records its purpose,
identity, and objectives. Therefore, to understand our roles as
leaders in our businesses, it helps to understand how our
organizations came to exist. Consider the picture on the following page.

This picture depicts how most organizations come into
being. A need is identified that an entrepreneur believes can be
met by creating a new business. The entrepreneur is often an
innovator who believes he or she can meet consumer needs

ORGANIZATIONAL "BEING"...

Need -   What is or will be needed by others

Vision -   Commitment to meet the need

Mission - Unique purpose fundamental to how the need will be met

Goals -   What must be done to achieve the purpose

Tasks -   What must get done to meet goals

Skills -   What is needed to get tasks done

better than what is currently available. To pursue development of the business, the entrepreneur develops a business plan. It explains

a. the consumer need;
b. the commitment the organization will make to meet it (vision);
c. how this commitment is unique to the industry (mission);
d. what results are expected in the first five-year timeframe (goals);
e. and, what resources, such as capital, equipment, and people, are needed to start the operation (tasks and skills).

Notice that the effective leadership cycle defined in Chapter 4 has leaders develop an understanding of their organizations similar to how it was established. Some may argue that not all new businesses are established with this level of planning, and I would agree. However, if investors, loans, or other working capital must be obtained prior to getting the business going, a business plan will be required.

The next diagram titled "Organizational Process," shows how the people in organizations are linked to the need the entrepreneur of a business has identified. It flows from the bottom up and summarizes organizations in the following (mouthful) manner:

> *Our employees use their skills to do the tasks designed to accomplish established goals, which must be successfully completed to realize our organizations' missions and fulfill the visionary commitments made to meet the needs of the consumers.*

ORGANIZATIONAL PROCESS

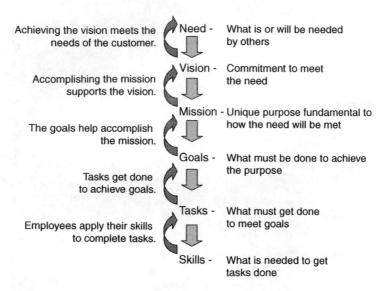

Achieving the vision meets the needs of the customer.

Need - What is or will be needed by others

Accomplishing the mission supports the vision.

Vision - Commitment to meet the need

The goals help accomplish the mission.

Mission - Unique purpose fundamental to how the need will be met

Tasks get done to achieve goals.

Goals - What must be done to achieve the purpose

Employees apply their skills to complete tasks.

Tasks - What must get done to meet goals

Skills - What is needed to get tasks done

By meeting customer needs, an entrepreneur hopes to achieve the visualized goals and ultimately to attain the predicted results. The founder strives for his or her business to supply exactly what is needed to every person seeking its products or services. However, like our team members, consumers are unique individuals who have personal opinions about what they need and how their needs should be met. Because of the individual nature of "needs," gaps will exist between what some consumers want and what the organization provides. As an example, consider the soft drink industry. There are about 500 different types of soft drinks available to Americans, indicative of the varied tastes of individuals.

Consequently, companies invest time and energy researching how they can better meet the needs of consumers. In doing so, they are trying to reduce the gap between what consumers want and what they provide. The results of this research are often included in organizations' strategic plans. The plans draw upon the conclusions of the research to establish specific organizational goals. In an effort to meet the goals, tasks are changed and employee skills are retooled. Through this process, more gaps can come into existence. It is a cycle that continually brings about organizational and personal change—back to Getting Real!

The complexity of organizational leadership lies in trying to identify the different types of "gaps" that exist

- if the founder misidentified the consumer needs;
- if the leadership's vision does not address all elements of those needs;
- if the mission falls short of supporting the vision;
- if the goals or tasks are incomplete;
- if the employees do not or cannot achieve those goals.

The organization will fail to be its best. In fact, it may fail, period. To help grasp where the organizational gaps exist, I envision it something like this:

ORGANIZATIONAL WORK GAPS

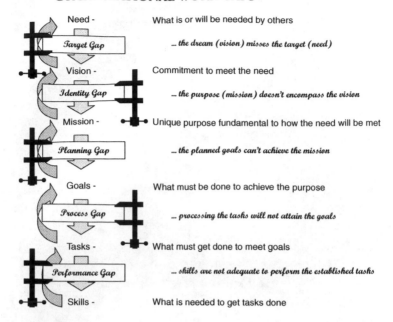

Need -	What is or will be needed by others
Target Gap	*... the dream (vision) misses the target (need)*
Vision -	Commitment to meet the need
Identity Gap	*... the purpose (mission) doesn't encompass the vision*
Mission -	Unique purpose fundamental to how the need will be met
Planning Gap	*... the planned goals can't achieve the mission*
Goals -	What must be done to achieve the purpose
Process Gap	*... processing the tasks will not attain the goals*
Tasks -	What must get done to meet goals
Performance Gap	*... skills are not adequate to perform the established tasks*
Skills -	What is needed to get tasks done

Interestingly, business leaders spend large amounts of money each year trying to identify and close these gaps, because they recognize that the potential of the organization lies in eliminating them. This is supported by the fact that over each of the past several years, U. S. companies have spent well over a quarter of a billion dollars for operational management consulting assistance. Although the organization likely did not hire these consultants for "gap reduction," many consulting services are engaged for that purpose. Organizations obtain consultants to assist in marketing studies (target gap), research and development (identity gap), strategic planning (planning gap), re-engineering (process gap), performance management and continued education (performance gap). Each activity is focused on compressing organizational gaps.

An additional complication to gap identification and reduction is that technology is accelerating the speed of change.

Consider the changes in cellular phone technology discussed earlier. Cell phone use grew from 38 million users in 1996 to over 100 million users in 2000. This is a 163 percent growth in only 4 years. How businesses introduced the use of cellular phone technology during this period of growth could have either broadened or closed organizational gaps, depending on how it was utilized. Thus, an organization's ability to succeed in the future will be directly linked to the ability of its leaders and employees to identify gaps, modify its vision, mission, and strategy, and change rapidly.

This requires unity in the efforts of all an organization's employees. For our employees to be unified to achieve organizational success, "success" for our businesses must be defined. Like the questions we raised in Get Together, we need to ask questions about staff knowledge of our organizations.

- Do our employees understand the mission and purpose of our organizations?
- Do they see the link between the jobs they come to work to perform each day and the goals of the company?
- Do they have input on how to perform their job tasks to maximize their contribution to the business?
- Are they aware of the performance gaps between their skills and what the organization needs accomplished?

As their leaders, we must ensure each of our employees can answer "yes" to these questions. If they cannot, we should not expect an unfailing commitment to, or intense passion for, our organizations' success.

Our organizations were started for a purpose. We not only need to understand their original purpose, but also how that purpose has evolved to the present. This history can help us identify how the organizational structure and tasks came to exist. It can also help us identify gaps between what is desired of the organization and what is actually occurring. However, this knowledge will only help us if we can engage employee skills and efforts to close the gaps. Therefore, the next chapter discusses how we can use the business tools introduced above to direct and unite staff.

> *Never let the future disturb you. You will meet it, if you have to, with the same weapons of reason which today arm you against the present.*
>
> *Marcus Aurelius Antonius*

18 | Use the Tools— Engage the People

CONSIDER HOW YOU WOULD FEEL IF YOU WERE TOLD YOU were going on a trip, but were not given any information about where you were going, when you were going to get there, or by what means you would be traveling. Unless it were planned by someone we deeply trusted, most of us would find it difficult to get excited about such a trip. We would be apprehensive or anxious, maybe—but not excited. What if on this trip you are given tasks to help you reach the destination, but you have no idea how your efforts contribute to the journey? If a wrong turn is taken or you are not on schedule, you will be clueless. Only those who know where you are headed and when you need to get there can identify whether you are on course and on time. Additionally, you would be helpless to assist in correcting problems. As the trip progresses, you are likely to wonder if there was a plan and feel very frustrated by the failure to reach your destination—wherever it is.

I believe this is analogous to how many organizations operate. Employees feel that a leader somewhere in the company has a plan that is being executed; or they believe that regardless of whether a plan exists or not, the company will operate as it always has. Either way, they do not view what they do each day as vital and important to the organization.

The last chapter presented the tools of vision statements, mission statements, and strategic plans as written methods of giving an organization its identity. The documents should clearly establish our organizations' destination, define the route by which we will arrive at that destination, and identify signposts needed to ensure the correct course with timetables maintained on our journey. As with any tools, having them and knowing how to use them are two very different things.

Think of a vision statement as a picture of a beautiful house that you want to build. The mission statement is the house's floor plan. The strategic plan and its goals represent the blueprints, materials, and tools needed to build the house to the floor plan's design. Now, suppose you frame and hang the picture of the house on a tree where you want it built. Then, you stack the materials, tools, blueprints, and floor plan beneath the picture. However, you never hire a building contractor or skilled laborers to use these items to build the house. How effective are they? The vision of your house cannot be realized unless the tools and materials you have provided are used. As importantly, they must be used by people who have seen the picture of the house they are building and can follow the blueprints to complete it successfully.

Similarly, when the vision, mission, and strategy of an organization are only understood by its leaders, they are as ineffective as the tools, materials, and blueprints for our house when they are stacked beneath a tree. Regardless of how well these tools define the organization's purpose and direction, they are ineffectual unless everyone in the business uses them.

Unfortunately, leaders often establish goals for their organizations in response to their customers or competition, without involving their employees. The rapid pace of change in our global economy requires decisive action and it is believed that time cannot be spent entertaining employee opinion or input. The goals require immediate improvement, i.e., change of employee activity. However, all the employees ever really understand is that they are expected to do something different. The goals are often elusive and they feel no emotional connection or personal motivation to change to achieve them.

A friend of mine was employed by a manufacturing company that suffered this type of disconnect between leadership goals and employee involvement whenever change was expected. To the employees, the leaders would adopt whatever was fashionable in leadership literature or marketed as industry innovations. They felt they were constantly asked to change for no significant reason and would actually respond to the expectations by saying, "This too shall pass." They did not understand the purpose of the changes and had no stake in achieving the goals. One such project was to reduce waste and improve the quality of items produced in each phase of manufacturing. The employees were not asked how to accomplish this. Instead, they were presented with a list of changes they were to make. Additionally, the paperwork required from each manufacturing segment grew significantly. The employees believed this extra work would only be used against them when the changes failed to yield results. One day, the employees actually distributed a customized version of the following story throughout the company. It expressed how they felt about changes introduced by their management.

> *Our company management decided to have a canoe race against our major competitor. Both teams practiced long and hard to reach peak performance before the race. On the big day, the competition's team won by a mile. Our company's leaders, very discouraged and depressed, decided to investigate the reason for the crushing defeat. A management team made up of senior executives was formed to investigate and recommend appropriate action. Their conclusion was that the competition's team had eight people rowing and one person steering, while our team had eight people steering and one person rowing. So senior management hired a*

consulting company and paid them a large amount of money to determine what action should be taken.

The consultants advised that too many people were steering the boat, while not enough people were rowing. To prevent another loss to the competition, our rowing team's structure was totally reorganized to four Steering Supervisors, three Steering Managers and one Vice President of Steering.

They also implemented a new performance system that would give the one person rowing the boat greater incentive to work harder. It was called the "Rowing Team Incentive Program." The program called for the rower to attend endless meetings, rower training, and rower attitude-improvement events. There were future plans to get new paddles, canoes, and other equipment. There was also discussion of providing the rower extra vacation days for practices and bonuses for performance, but that was dismissed as ineffective and unnecessary.

The next year, the competition won by two miles.

Humiliated, our management laid off the rower for poor performance, halted development of the new canoe, sold the paddles, canceled all capital investments for new equipment, and had a 10 percent reduction in our workforce. The money saved was distributed to the company's senior executives as bonuses. Our company's management is so creative.

The employees felt that when goals needed to be achieved in the organization, they should be involved in how to change to ensure success. They knew their jobs and wanted to be recognized as the people who could provide the greatest insights into what would improve the company. When that involvement wasn't sought, they looked at the entire process as another canoe race with leaders defining what needed to change and expecting them to do it, whether or not it would improve things.

We must recognize that for our plans to succeed, communication and involvement of our employees is mandatory. In fact, just as we discovered for personal change, recognition that a change is needed and an urgency to move forward must be shared by our entire team. When leaders alone believe change is needed, while the followers disagree or resist the change efforts, the desired results are almost never achieved. Equally destructive to organizations is an environment in which the employees feel that change is needed, but that feeling is not shared by those in leadership roles. There must be unity acknowledging the need for change. Without it, organizations become frozen and unable to respond to the businesses' needs in a meaningful and constructive manner.

Certainly, time does not support group consensus on every decision made or change project established by organizational leaders. Yet, the employees need to "buy-in" to them to yield the support necessary to succeed. That is why it is so important for our foundational tools to be clear, shared, and understood. Leadership decisions and directions are made with these organizational objectives in mind. Therefore, the tools will always provide the answer to why every activity is needed for the business.

How, then, do organizational leaders make sure their tools are well constructed and available to their employees? Each of us must start where we are. In some cases, our organizations may have all of these tools. We need to use them and expand upon them to create customized tools for our team. Our team's vision, mission, and strategy connect the work that our group must accomplish to the achievement of organizational goals. If our organizations do not utilize these tools, it remains our obligation to provide our team the tools they need to succeed.

Suppose our organization has a vision and mission statement that is

A
Vision
&
Mission
Creator

well scripted and placed in prominent places. Unfortunately, that is the extent of their usefulness. There is no written strategic plan or specific goals established for the business. We might undertake steps similar to the following to integrate the organization's vision and mission tools into customized tools for our team:

1. Meet with our team to review the vision and mission statements of our organization.
2. Following the organizational "being" flow, we need to record
   • Who are our area's customers?
   • What are their needs?
   • How does meeting their needs support our organization's vision and mission?
3. Work with our team to develop vision and mission statements for our area of responsibility.
4. Define activities that are critical to successfully achieving our mission and vision
5. Identify the strengths, weaknesses, opportunities, threats, and issues of our team.
6. List the top five goals that will help our team improve.

Appendix B provides a set of detailed worksheets to assist us in this effort. The worksheets should be completed by each member of staff. We should then work with staff members to develop a single team worksheet and plan for the group. This process links the vision of our organization to the goals we establish for not only the team, but also for individual team members. It therefore necessitates candid input and involvement of our team members—i.e., getting real and getting together. We must expect every employee who reports to us to understand the tools and to use them to support their decisions and efforts. This is where individual performance management becomes critically important.

19 | Employee Performance Management

I HAVE ALWAYS FELT THAT THE BEST WAY TO DESCRIBE AN organization is that it is a group of people brought together for a specific purpose. We utilize business communication tools, like mission statements, to share that purpose with our employees. Each organizational unit or team has job responsibilities designed to assist in achieving the purpose of the business. We define goals and measures for the team to unify the individual skills and efforts of its members. We now need to personalize each individual's role in helping the team succeed. This is accomplished through performance management.

The performance management processes of an organization provide the communication that links individual performance to team and business goals. The following picture is a simple illustration of the connection between our organizational tools, team tools, and each employee:

Organization Vision, Mission, & Strategic Plan
⬇
Organizational Goals, Measures, & Timelines
⬇
Team Vision, Mission, & Strategic Plan
⬇
Team Goals, Measures, & Timelines
⬇
Individual Goals, Measures, & Timelines

As illustrated, performance management requires us to set individual goals, measures, and timelines for our employees.

By getting together, we acquire knowledge of employee skills and career objectives. We need to use this information to establish specific goals that will help them improve their team performance and grow professionally. In organizations that have established performance appraisal standards, the communication of this information is provided in writing. For the appraisal process to be effective, organizational performance management procedures should exist. These procedures should be provided by HR to help all organizational leaders consistently identify and document employee performance goals and needed improvements. In organizations where such procedures exist, we need to develop an applicable knowledge of them. If the organization does not have a standardized performance management process, Appendix D provides a simple form that we can use as a template for developing our own written standard.

Our written assessment of past performance and the goals we establish for the future must clearly connect the individual efforts of our staff members to our team and organizations' purpose. Performance communications should be direct, fact-based, and supported by examples. Although we should practice this in all performance-related communications, it is especially important when our assessment is provided in writing. An effective leader, for example, will not write performance evaluation comments such as "Joe is an easygoing, team-oriented member of our staff." Comments such as these are not only opinions, they describe an impression of Joe, not his performance. In contrast, an effective

leader will state, "On project XYZ, Joe completed his assigned tasks on time, within budget, and with results that exceeded projected targets." Likewise, goals should not be generic. "Become familiar with the company's financial processes," does not establish a specific, measurable goal. Although many goals are written in this manner, a better directive would be, "Complete training with a senior accountant and score above 80 percent on a test of the organization's general ledger accounts by January 1, 20xx." This language describes specifically what is to be accomplished, who is to be involved, and when it is to be completed. Every goal should provide this information.

During performance management training, two questions are raised consistently:

1. "How do you establish specific goals for employees whose job responsibilities are repetitive?," and
2. "How do you assess goals that were not completed due to a shift or change in business focus?"

First, I believe every person can improve the quality of his or her job tasks or improve the skills that he or she has to offer the organization. Additionally, repetition does not ensure improvement and getting real means no one performs at a level of perfection. Improvements can be made in every position, regardless of how repetitive they are. Determining what goals are appropriate requires a leader to ask questions specific to the individual's performance. Consider the following examples:

- If an employee is processing 50 repetitive actions in an hour, what could they do to make the average 51? "Improve your average parts per hour production from the current rate of 50 to 51 over the next 12 months."
- How can this employee help their teammates improve their performance? "Compare in writing how 50 parts per

hour can be accomplished by teammates currently averag-
ing 45. The document created should identify specific
changes to approach or improvement of skills you believe
would assist others. It is to be confidential and submitted
for review by June 20, 20xx."

- If his work rate is constrained by a task before him in the
process, can he make suggestions on how to improve the
process? "Spend one week working in XYZ group, evaluating their processes and procedures, and offer performance
suggestions you believe would improve their output to our
team. This assessment will be confidential and completed
within the next six months."

The manager of a data entry center was frustrated when
he was asked by his HR manager to write specific objectives
for employees who repetitively entered data into the business
system. To help him think beyond the repetition, the HR
manager asked him if his employees were performing their
jobs to perfection. He was somewhat offended by the question
and responded, "No! Nobody is perfect." He was then asked
how he knew the employees were doing their jobs well. He
said the employees completed all the work that was given to
them each day. He was asked if he tracked error rates of the
information entered. He replied that he did not. He was asked
if simply completing work ensured quality. He said he had no
way of knowing if the work was accurate, just that it was done.
When he was asked how he could know that it was done
accurately, he said, "Short of looking at every document
entered, I don't know." The HR manager realized that this
manager had not established any innovative mechanisms to
measure the quality of his employees' work. With the HR
manager's help, this leader established some production statistics, such as average entries per hour per employee. Additionally,
the manager established an audit process to check 10 pieces of

work from each of his employees per week. Over time, this audit process would provide him the information needed to assess the quality of each employee's work.

As the story illustrates, often leaders have to complete additional job tasks to measure employee performance. Leadership is, after all, work. These tasks are important as they provide a consistent mechanism for measuring the work product of each employee. By identifying how he or she can improve, individualized performance goals and expectations can be established. As emphasized, our leadership path ensures that each of these goals, if accomplished, will improve the individual's contribution to our organization. Additionally, performance to these goals determines success.

The second question is how performance can be measured if the priorities of the organization render employee performance goals worthless to the business. For example, suppose a goal was given to an employee to improve his or her task productivity by 10 percent within the year. However, 5 months after this goal is given, the machine on which the employee works is replaced. The employee now has a new set of tasks and processes to learn and the prior goal does not apply. Thus, the original improvement goal was no longer valid. The leader must react to this change and establish new goals that represent what is needed from the employee in transitioning to the new machine. At appraisal time, the performance of the employee on the original goal states that the goal was changed because of machine replacement. Then, the leader should record how the employee responded to and performed through the change.

There are always specific things individuals can do to improve themselves or their contributions to a team. The key to useful performance management is knowing what improvements will benefit each individual and then clearly articulating each person's goals. When each person accomplishes their goals, improvement will be recognized for our team.

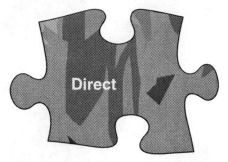

We underscored the importance of communication to our relational effectiveness in Chapter 13 and our need to learn to manage conflict in Chapter 14. In managing the performance of employee efforts for our organizations, these skills are critical, especially when employee performance is not meeting the organization's needs. We illustrated how to specify goals and assess those goals in a direct manner. Suppose Joe, who worked on project XYZ, failed to achieve the goals established for him. Having measured his performance, his leader would provide to him a communication similar to the following: "On project XYZ, Joe failed to meet his responsibilities to his team by being late and over budget on three of his four deliverables. His efforts also failed to meet the established standards of quality set for these tasks."

Addressing poor performance often leads to difficult conflict situations. Nonetheless, they are situations we must recognize are a critical responsibility of leadership. As much as we may hate to admit it, the observation that "a chain is only as strong as its weakest link" sums up a team's ability to reach its potential. One person who is not passionate about what he or she is doing, or who is not committed to serving the organization's goals, will prevent the team from performing at its best. Strengthening or changing behaviors that cause team members to be perceived as "weak links" or, when necessary, removing poor performers from the chain, is the job of a leader. Please, do not misunderstand this statement: No individual should ever be categorized as a "weak link." Every individual deserves to be valued. However, the behaviors of each person are ultimately his or her own responsibility and his or her choice.

As leaders, we must respond decisively when those choices limit or adversely affect the team.

Unfortunately, this is an area where many leaders fall short. Although it is hard to confront others with negative information, it is even harder to document that negative information in a clear and direct manner. However, to be relationally effective we must address "weak link" behaviors on our teams or we risk losing our strong employees.

Even more troubling is that very few leaders try to determine if there is an addressable cause of "weak link" performance. Employees who lack the skills necessary to perform the tasks requested of them are likely to be unsuccessful in meeting their leader's expectations. Similarly, employees who have the skills, but do not like what they are doing, are not going to deliver their best efforts. Only by knowing employees on a personal level will we be equipped to determine the reasons poor performance exists. We must also have this same knowledge to understand how to help our employees improve. We need to Get Together first.

A young woman was hired into a medium-size organization to work as a liaison for users in the information systems area. Her credentials were impressive and her understanding of both the business users' needs and technical documentation needs were demonstrated in every project with which she was involved. Unfortunately, her approach was aggressive and both business and technical members began to dread working on projects to which she was assigned. Everyone conceded that her knowledge and assertiveness accomplished good things for the organization; she simply did not work well in engaging people. Her leader discussed directly with her both the positive and negative aspects of her performance. Together they identified a needed position in the organization that would use her skills, while reducing her need to engage others. Although she needed to recognize the effects of her behaviors on others and improve them, they were not as critical in her new position. By fully understanding this individual's strengths and weaknesses, the leader was able to match her skills with a job that allowed her the opportunity to succeed.

Sadly, sometimes ending our work affiliation with a staff member is the only course of action. There are times when either our employees do not want to change or simply cannot change in the manner required of them. If we find we have employees who cannot accomplish what is necessary for success in their role, despite the help and clear direction we offer, they should not be surprised when they are removed from the organization's chain. While this may seem like a harsh response, it is a reality for every leader.

The key characteristic we must maintain throughout the process of separation is respectfulness. Being respectful of the person leaving the organization is necessary to ensure our efforts for relational effectiveness are not compromised. We should always consider an employee's effort for the  organization when determining how a separation with him or her is to be accomplished. For example, an employee who has worked faithfully for the organization for years, but has been unable to adapt to organizational changes, should not leave the company under the same circumstances as someone who, in his or her nine months with the organization, just did not want to do the work. We need to work with our HR professionals and plan the appropriate course of action specific to each employee separation. Whether we offer nothing, outplacement assistance, continuing education, or a severance package, our efforts should be reflective of the employee's overall efforts for the organization. This is not only important for the dignity of the individual, but also to support the morale of those who remain.

Last, we should never ignore the communication needed with other team members when a separation occurs. Too often, leaders choose to move on as if nothing has happened. Although separations are not a matter for extensive discussion, having an employee there one day and gone the next without saying anything to their teammates will hurt our relational credibility. Even if our team recognized substandard performance in the departing individual, they need to hear the separation news from us. Simply explaining that the separation took place and that members of the team can discuss any concerns they have about the matter with us privately, has a tremendously positive impact on refocusing our team. Do remember though, we will discuss their concerns and feelings, not the performance of their former coworker.

We must ensure that employees understand what our organization's expectations are of teams, what measures will be used to keep us on track, and how important individual success is to teams. The goals we establish for them individually have the same characteristics. They are clearly described in terms of their importance to the team or individual's skill growth and each goal has measurable evidence of its achievement. This is where our efforts to Get Together with our staff members are most valuable. It helps us establish goals to improve what they are doing today with those that will grow their skills for tomorrow. Accordingly, we do not limit the goals of staff to activities related only to their current responsibilities. Rather, we evaluate how we can help individuals grow skills important to them that may ultimately expand their value to the organization in the future. For example, just because an employee does not engage in public speaking in their current position, does not mean that we should not consider a goal of completing a speech class for individual self-improvement. We must remember, success is defined as achieving an established goal. As leaders, we establish the continuity between what needs to be accomplished for organizational success and what team members want to achieve personally. When the career goals of each individual can be reached while accomplishing the goals of the organization, leadership effectiveness has been attained. The leader will have successfully put together all of the pieces of the leadership puzzle.

20 | Bringing It All Together

At the beginning of this book, I summarized the goal of effective leadership development: to consistently exhibit behaviors that positively influence and unify others while improving the business skills needed to achieve organizational goals. However, as Antoine de Saint-Exupery said, "A goal without a plan is just a wish." The purpose of *Get Real! Get Together! Get Success!* is to provide a plan for developing leadership effectiveness. The approach presented within this book is rather simple: to establish our leadership focuses from an organizational viewpoint, then work faithfully to improve our character, relationships, and team accomplishments. The approach needs to be simple, because actually developing leadership effectiveness is difficult.

Although each of us is unique and brings different skills and talents to leadership roles, we must share two principles if this plan is to be beneficial to us.

First, we must abhor complacency. We need to develop a passion for continually improving ourselves, helping others set and achieve their career goals, and contributing positively to the quest of our organization's vision. If we allow ourselves to be complacent with how things are, we will fail to realize our potential. Unfortunately, our complacency as leaders will also limit the capabilities of our teams and our organizations. Thus, growing in leadership effectiveness requires a commitment to improvement—and improvement always requires change.

Thus, our second shared principle is that change in life is inevitable. As leaders, we must accept it, manage it, and at times, embrace it. We must do this personally, relationally, and especially professionally. Research has shown that if change at the organizational level is to succeed, it must be accomplished by the individual members of a group. Therefore, we not only need to understand how individual change is accomplished, but also be adept at managing it. By learning and consistently applying a change management strategy in our personal improvement efforts, we can become more proficient with its use as leaders. Additionally, we must be able to identify the resistance factors that are most common during the change process. By doing so, we can respond in an assertive manner when resistance to needed change emerges.

Our responsibility to our organizations is to accomplish job tasks at a quality standard that surpasses organizational needs. Since we cannot do all job tasks ourselves, we must get them done through our employees. We must know how to communicate with them as individuals and as a team. Helen Keller said it best: "Alone we can do so little; together we can do so much." To be effective leaders, we must use the ideas of everyone on our team and unite their efforts for the organization. To lead each individual, we focus on helping them understand the expectations, challenges, and measures to which we will hold them accountable. Furthermore, they must recognize our commitment to share organizational knowledge and willingness to help them capitalize on their strengths, overcome their weaknesses, and grow personally. They must acknowledge that we are people of positive character who ask no more of them than we do of ourselves. When our employees respond to meet goals we have established with their best efforts, our leadership influence will be effective.

When we put together all of the pieces of the leadership puzzle and lead our teams to achieve all their goals, we have achieved success. It would be wonderful if each goal before us could be accomplished by doing everything in precisely the same way as the goal we just successfully achieved. Unfortunately, the speed of change in the business world and in individuals' lives requires us to adapt and rework our plans, constantly and rapidly. The picture of success for our organizations changes, and to meet this challenge, we must continually refine our skills and strengthen our relationships with team members. When circumstances change, effective leaders react innovatively and impress upon their staff the need to respond similarly. The volatility of the business environment requires this type of unified reaction. Ultimately, the success of our organizations will be measured by how well we deliver the products or services required of us by our customers. When we fail, we must work with our customers and our team to determine what we need to change in order to improve. And when we succeed, we celebrate together.

The strategy of Get Real! Get Together! Get Success! can be applied, whether we are new to leadership or have been leaders for some time, and to be its most effective, it should be passed on to everyone entering a leadership role. Many leaders must improve in this area. We must work to develop new leaders. When we promote an individual to a supervisory or management role, we need to place them immediately on the path to effective leadership development. We must let each person know that although he or she should be proud of their achievements, leading others requires a new focus. In fact, it requires a focus in three different areas: personal effectiveness (Get Real), relational effectiveness, (Get Together), and organizational effectiveness (Get Success).

We should outline honestly for each new leader the role that behaviors and attitudes play in their personal effectiveness. If we are aware of potential issues in this area, we should suggest books, training, or coaching to help them improve. We can help them compare needed leadership skills to the skills they have demonstrated in their careers thus far, and develop training plans and goals specifically to help them enhance and develop as leaders. We can help them assess the relationships they have with others and suggest tools or workshops that will improve their rapport and influence with their new staff. Most importantly, we can develop standardized training on the purpose of our organization, its history, and its current goals. We can share with each new leader how their group and the tasks for which they are responsible assist the business in achieving its goals. Every leader we place on the path to effectiveness helps us become better leaders for our organizations. When leaders emphasize to their employees the importance of getting real, getting together and getting success, the workplace begins to transform. But, it all starts with us—the leaders.

The most effective way we can approach our leadership responsibilities is by evaluating everything done from an organizational perspective. We establish personal skill and behavior goals that will improve our skills, our contributions to our organizations, and our influence on our employees. We are driven by a commitment to reach our potential (Get Real). We work to know each of our coworkers and strengthen our relationships by using reliable communication skills. We confront conflict situations directly and provide each employee the opportunity to succeed. Additionally, our employees understand our responsibilities as leaders to unify them into a team

(Get Together). Our remaining challenge is to fight through the ever-changing landscape of the business jungle with our teams to help achieve the purposes of our organizations (Get Success). With courage, commitment, dependability, and enthusiasm, we must create the unity necessary for our teams to reach our destinations. Although constantly changing and developing, we work in a unified manner to attain our goals—personally and organizationally. And as we strive for leadership effectiveness, our greatest reward will be the relationships we develop along the way.

Effective leadership and success share an important reality: Neither is a destination at which we can arrive and rest; therefore, we should ensure we have fun together on the journey.

> *Consider how hard it is to change yourself and you'll understand what little chance you have in trying to change others.*
>
> *Jacob Braude*

Appendix A

The following table lists groups of character traits. Each box contains contrasting characteristics. Please highlight ten boxes that contain character traits you feel are most important to leadership effectiveness. Then, circle the trait in the box that you feel best describes my leadership. Additionally, if you feel a trait describes me that hampers or interferes with my leadership effectiveness please circle that trait as well. Please note that this is requested to help me improve and is to be confidential. Please do not provide your name or other identifying marks. Be assured that there will be no attempt to determine the source of feedback provided. Therefore, your candor is appreciated. Thank you!

receptive or indifferent	cooperative or uncooperative	loyal or disloyal	conscientious or careless
ambitious or unmotivated	demanding or easy-going	malicious or kind	imaginative or unimaginative
argumentative or harmonious	dependable or undependable	mean or nice	trustworthy or untrustworthy
arrogant or humble	determined or unsure	moody or even-tempered	courageous or spineless

attentive or inattentive	disagreeable or agreeable	obnoxious or pleasant	independent or team oriented
boastful or modest	discreet or tactless	reflective or superficial	unfriendly or friendly
bold or faint-hearted	dishonest or honest	resourceful or unimaginative	creative or unoriginal
bossy or gentle	enthusiastic or apathetic	respectful or disrespectful	self-controlled or hot-headed
bully or champion	fair or unfair	rude or polite	hypocritical or genuine
brave or cowardly	decisive or indecisive	sarcastic or diplomatic	optimistic or pessimistic
calm or agitated	generous or stingy	self-centered or selfless	consistent or inconsistent
caring or uncaring	gullible or smart	self-confident or timid	compassionate or callous
cautious or precautious	happy or unhappy	selfish or unselfish	temperamental or mild-mannered
cheerful or distressing	wise or foolish	sincere or insincere	diplomatic or autocratic
conceited or modest	supportive or unsupportive	stubborn or accommodating	helpful or unhelpful

Appendix B

Team Operating Principles—PART I

Original: *date*
Last Revision: *date*

Unit/Team Name: _____

Team Leader: _____

Member Name: _____

Team Member Skills: *(The areas the team member can/wants to help this team. Use an additional sheet if needed.)*

1. _____
   _____
   _____
   _____
   _____
   _____

2. _____
   _____
   _____
   _____
   _____
   _____

3. _____

4. _____

Team Operating Principles — PART I
Original: *date*
Last Revision: *date*

About Me: *To help the team understand you, list what motivates you in your work. Then list your "pet peeves"—things that other people do that frustrate you and could cause conflict.*

I am motivated by...

1. _____
2. _____
3. _____
4. _____
5. _____

I get annoyed when others...

1. _____
2. _____
3. _____
4. _____
5. _____

Team's Behavioral Ground Rules: *(List what you feel are important ways for members to behave toward each other and as a team.)*

1. _____
2. _____
3. _____
4. _____
5. _____
6. _____
7. _____
8. _____
9. _____
10. _____

Team Operating Principles—PART I

Original: *date*
Last Revision: *date*

Conflict Management: *What conflicts occur among team members and what steps will the members take to resolve them?*

_____

_____

_____

_____

_____

_____

_____

_____

_____

_____

_____

Team Operating Principles—PART II

Original: *date*
Last Revision: *date*

Unit/Team Name: _____

Team Leader: _____

Team Members:

1.	2.
3.	4.
5.	6.
7.	8.
9.	10.

Team Member Skills: *(The areas the team member can/wants to help this team)*

1. _____
2. _____
3. _____
4. _____
5. _____
6. _____
7. _____
8. _____
9. _____
10. _____

Team's Behavioral Ground Rules:

1. _____
2. _____
3. _____
4. _____
5. _____
6. _____
7. _____
8. _____
9. _____
10. _____

Team Operating Principles—PART II
Original: *date*
Last Revision: *date*

Conflict Management: *What conflicts occur among team members and what steps will the members take to resolve them?*

_____

_____

_____

_____

_____

_____

_____

_____

_____

_____

_____

_____

_____

_____

_____

_____

_____

_____

_____

Appendix C

Team Tool Worksheet

Section 1—Our Organization

Our organization has established the following vision statement, mission statement, and strategic goals. If the business has not established formal statements or goals, our team will develop them together.

Organization's Vision: _____

_____

_____

Organization's Mission:

_____

_____

_____

_____

Organization's Strategic Goals:

1. _____
2. _____
3. _____
4. _____
5. _____

Team Tool Worksheet

Section 2—About Our Team

Each member of our team will complete this section of the worksheet.

Based on the mission, vision, and goals of our organization, what is our team's purpose?

_____
_____
_____
_____

Based on our organization's vision and mission statements and our stated team's purpose, what is our group's vision?

_____
_____
_____

Who are our customers? A. _____

B. _____

C. _____

D. _____

Team Tool Worksheet

Section 2—About Our Team

What are their needs?

A. _____

_____

_____

B. _____

_____

_____

C. _____

_____

_____

D. _____

_____

_____

How does meeting their needs support our organization's vision and mission statements?

_____

_____

_____

_____

Team Tool Worksheet

Section 2—About Our Team

If each of our customers were to write a tribute about the products or services we provide to them, what would we want each of them to say?

A. _____
_____
_____
_____

B. _____
_____
_____
_____

C. _____
_____
_____
_____

D. _____
_____
_____
_____

Team Tool Worksheet

Section 2—About Our Team

Based on what we want our customers to say about us, what is our group's mission?

_____

_____

_____

_____

_____

_____

Team Tool Worksheet

Section 3—Critical Success Factors

Consider the following aspects of our group and then answer each question on the list.

a. The procedures we have in place for our unit...
b. The processes we use to meet our customer's needs...
c. Our team's structure, leadership, and skills...

1. What has to go right for our team to be successful each day?

2. What are the worst things that can go wrong for our team?

3. What are the basic goals and objectives of our team? i.e., What is it the organization pays our team to accomplish?

4. What problems keep us from meeting our team's goals and objectives?

5. What has kept the problems from being solved?

6. What would it take for us to become three times more productive?

7. Who in the company depends on us? Who do we depend on?

8. What does management need to know about your job that it doesn't know?

9. Is our unit organized for growth? (Why or why not?)

10. Is our group prepared to accept and implement changes rapidly? (Why or why not?)

Team Tool Worksheet

Section 3—Critical Success Factors

Consider your responses to the questions above and identify what is critical to our team's success? (i.e., What are the top five activities in which favorable results are absolutely necessary for our team to achieve its mission?)

1. _____

2. _____

3. _____

4. _____

5. _____

Team Tool Worksheet

Section 4—Our Team's SWOTI

Strengths, Weaknesses, Opportunities, Threats, and Issues

In this section we need to record the strengths, weaknesses, opportunities, threats, and issues of our group.

Strengths

What are the top five strengths of our team that support our critical success factors?

1. _____
2. _____
3. _____
4. _____
5. _____

Weaknesses

What are the five weaknesses that most limit or inhibit our team's ability to attain our critical success factors?

1. _____
2. _____
3. _____
4. _____
5. _____

Opportunities

In evaluating our critical success factors, what opportunities do we have to do something new that would improve/accelerate progress toward them?

1. _____
2. _____

3. _____
4. _____
5. _____

Team Tool Worksheet

Section 4—Our Team's SWOTI

Strengths, Weaknesses, Opportunities, Threats, and Issues

Threats

Given the critical success factor, what could happen that would keep our team from being able to accomplish the factor's objectives?

1. _____
2. _____
3. _____
4. _____
5. _____

Issues

Are there any issues within our team that must be addressed before we will be able to meet our critical success factor's objectives?

1. _____
2. _____
3. _____
4. _____
5. _____

Team Tool Worksheet

Section 5—Our Team's Goals

Review our team's strengths, weaknesses, opportunities, threats, issues, and critical success factors. List what you believe to be the top five goals needed to establish team growth and improvement.

1. _____
2. _____
3. _____
4. _____
5. _____

Team Tool Worksheet

Section 6—Our Plan

Use the following form to suggest a plan of action you believe should be taken for each plan goal.

Goal:		
Project Leader: Team Members:		
Detailed Steps	Timeline	Benchmark Measures
1.		
2.		
3.		
4.		
5.		
6.		
7.		
8.		
9.		
10.		
What quantifies success? (Must be measurable)		

Appendix D

Performance Evaluation Form

Performance Assessment

Performance Evaluation For: _____

Evaluation Period: _____

Evaluation Date: _____

Completed By: _____

Evaluate the employee for each of the identified criteria using the following rating scale:

0—Not Applicable
1—Improvement Needed
2—Met Requirements of Job
3—Exceeded Requirements of Job

Where improvement is needed or exceeded the job requirements, provide specific examples of performance in the evaluation period that resulted in this rating. Comments suggesting improvements must be provided for each "1—Improvement Needed" rating. Comments should also be provided as coaching to assist the professional growth of the employee.

Criteria	Rating	Example and Comments
Demonstrated technical competence in job		
Understood and supported the organization's culture		
Completed assignments specific to current job responsibilities		
Demonstrated knowledge about the strategic direction of the organization and unit		
Made timely and accurate decisions		
Took responsibility for personal performance		
Sets relevant & measurable performance goals		
Exhibited a sense of urgency & self-motivation in accomplishing job tasks		
Identified/evaluated issues		
Investigated alternatives to improve performance		
Offered creative solutions to job related issues		
Was proactive in taking action to resolve issues or improve processes		
Embraced changes for self-improvement		
Verbal skills demonstrated the ability to clearly transmit information		
Communicated information necessary to keep staff, peers, and leaders informed		
Written communication was clear, concise, well researched, and accurate		
Worked well on team tasks/projects		
Established and/or maintained effective relationships		
Demonstrated a commitment to cooperation and teamwork		

Work was respected and valued by staff, peers, and leaders		
Demonstrated effective planning skills		
Prioritized tasks/projects in a practical & efficient manner		
Assessed performance in a direct and constructive manner		
Set measurable performance goals for others		

Performance Assessment Goals

Performance Evaluation for: _____

Evaluation Period: _____

Evaluation Date: _____

Completed By: _____

Prior Period Goals	Rating	Evaluation Comments

Next Period Goals	Measure of Success	Due Date

Bibliography and Recommended Reading

"A Journey in Time" by Seiko Watch Corporation: 2006. www.seikowatches.com/corporate/journey.asp

"A New Health Education Paradigm: Uncommon Thoughts about Common Matters" by Elbert D. Glover. *American Journal of Health Education,* 35(5). American Alliance for Health, Physical Education and Recreation: 2004.

"A Perspective on Team Building" by Dr. Jean Gordon. *Journal of American Academy of Business, Cambridge,* 2(1). Journal of American Academy of Business: 2002.

"Accelerating Executive Development: Hey, Coach..." by Susan Cramm & Thornton May. *Information Management & Computer Security,* 6(5). MCB UP Limited (MCB): 1998.

"Building Teams That Learn" by Paulo Vision Cunha & Maria Joao Lorus. *The Academy of Management Executive,* 14(1). Academy of Management: 2000.

"Caring Leadership: Secret and Path to Success" by Mary Ann Brandt. *Nursing Management,* 25(8). S-N Publications, Incorporated: 1994.

"Creativity in the Context of Team Diversity: Team Leader Perspectives" by Toby Marshall Egan. *Advances in Developing Human Resources*, 7(2). Sage Publications: 2005.

Developing The Leader Within You by John Maxwell. Injoy Inc.: 1993.

"Employee Turnover's $$ Cost" by Ron Hall. *Landscape Management*, 44(3). Advanstar Communications, Inc.: 2005.

"Engaging Employees in Achieving Corporate Goals" by Jennifer Schade. *Public Relations Strategist*. 10(4). Public Relations Society of America, Incorporated: 2004.

Failing Forward: How to Make the Most of Your Mistakes by John Maxwell. Nelson Business: 2000.

"From Engagement to Passion for Work: The Search for the Missing Person" by Ed Gubman. *HR Human Resource Planning*, 27(3). Human Resource Planning Society: 2004.

Generations at Work by Ron Zemke, Claire Raines & Bob Filipczak. AMACOM: 2000.

"Getting Real: Ten 'Truth Skills' to Enhance Emotional Connection, Intimacy and Well Being" by Susan Campbell. *Communities*, 113. Fellowship for Intentional Community: 2001.

"Getting Real: The Need for Genuine Leaders" by Linda Moran, Craig Perrin & Chris Blauth. *The Catalyst*, 34(3). National Council for Continuing Education & Training: 2005.

"Happy People, Happy Returns" by Matthew Boyle. *Fortune*, 153(1). Time Inc.: 2006.

"Honest to Goodness, Most of Us Lie: Yet Our Secrets and Lies Corrode Our Mental and Physical Health—Even if We Cross Our Fingers" by Bob Conder. *Calgary Herald*, Calgary Herald: 2002.

How to Win Friends and Influence People by Dale Carnegie. Pocket Books, Simon & Schuster Inc.: 1990.

"Individual Change Transition: Moving in Circles Can Be Good for You" by Erica French & Brian Delahaye. *Leadership & Organization Development Journal,* 17(7). MCB UP Limited (MCB): 1996.

"Inventory Imagines Future Phones" by *Wired News*: Apr 06, 2003. www.wired.com/news/technology/0,1282,58367,00.html

Jesus, CEO Using Ancient Wisdom for Visionary Leadership by Laurie Beth Jones. Hyperion: 1995.

Leadership by the Book: Tools to Transform Your Workplace by Ken Blanchard & Bill Hybels. William Morrow & Company Inc.: 1999.

"Leadership, Team Building, and Team Member Characteristics in High Performance Project Teams" by Anthony P. Ammeter & Janet M. Dukerich. *Engineering Management Journal,* 14(4). American Society for Engineering Management: 2002.

"Leadership: The Get-it-Together Profession" by Harlan Cleveland. *The Futurist,* 36(5). World Future Society: 2002.

"Lying: Deception in Human Affairs" by Bernard N. Meltzer. *The International Journal of Sociology and Social Policy,* 23(6/7). Barmarick Press: 2003.

"Managerial Quality, Team Success, and Individual Player Performance in Major League Baseball" by Lawrence M. Kahn. *Industrial & Labor Relations Review,* 46(3). Cornell University: 1993.

"Managing Strategic Relationships: The Key to Business Success" by Carol M. Sanchez. *The Academy of Management Executive,* 15(2). Academy of Management: 2001.

Merriam-Webster's Online by Merriam-Webster, Incorporated: 2006. www.m-w.com

Monday Morning Leadership by David Cottrell. Cornerstone Leadership Inst.: 2002.

"Motivation and Internal Relationship Are the Secret to Success" by Josef Busuttel. *Credit Management II, III,* Credit Management Ltd.: 2004.

"New Research Proves Interpersonal Skills Make High-Performing Managers; Study Shows That Building Effective Relationships Is Critical to Managerial Success" by Mackenzie Bartels, TRACOM Group. *Business Wire,* Business Wire: 2005.

On the Brink—The Life and Leadership of Norman Brinker by Norman Brinker & Donald T. Phillips. The Summit Publishing Group: 1996.

"Personal Change in the Information Age" by Michael Maccoby. *Research Technology Management,* 37(3). Industrial Research Institute, Incorporated: 1994.

"Research on Impacts of Team Leadership on Team Effectiveness" by Chia-Chen Kuo. *The Journal of American Academy of Business, Cambridge,* Journal of American Academy of Business, Cambridge: 2004.

"Secrets of High-Performing Executive Teams" by Jim McNerney. *Vital Speeches of the Day,* 72(11). City News Publishing Company: 2006.

"Seven Mistakes Leaders Make" by Joanne G. Sujansky. *Restaurant Hospitality.* Penton Publishing: 2004.

"Success Depends on Relationships: Ziglar". *Knight Ridder Tribune Business News,* The Times of India, distributed by Knight Ridder/Tribune Business News: 2005.

"Success in the Relationship Age: Building Quality Relationship Assets for Market Value Creation" by Jeremy Galbreath. *The TQM Magazine,* 14(1). MCB UP Limited (MCB): 2002.

"Team Captain's Perceptions of Athlete Leadership" by Martin Dupuis, Gordon A. Bloom & Todd M Loughead. *Journal of Sport Behavior,* 29(1). Journal of Sport Behavior, University of South Alabama: 2006.

"The Benefits of Frequent Positive Affect: Does Happiness Lead to Success?" by Sonja Lyubornirsky, Laura King, & Ed Diener. *Psychological Bulletin,* 131(6). American Psychological Association: 2005.

The Five Temptations of a CEO by Patrick Lencioni. Jossey-Bass: 1998.

The Goal by Eliyaha M. Goldratt & Jeff Cox. North River Press: 2004.

"The Historical Significance of Lying and Dissimulation" by Prez Zagorin. *Social Research,* 63(3). New School for Social Research, Graduate Faculty: 1996

The Leadership Pill: The Missing Ingredient in Motivating People Today by Ken Blanchard & Marc Muchnick. Free Press: 2003.

"The Mission Statement Is a Strategic Tool: When Used Properly" by John V. Mullane. *Management Decision,* 40(5/6). MCB UP Limited: 2002.

"The Nature of Athlete Leadership" by Todd M. Loughead, James Hardy, & Mark A. Eys. *Journal of Sports Behavior,* 29(2).

Journal of Sports Behavior, University of South Alabama: 2006.

The Purpose-Driven Life: What on Earth Am I Here For? by Rick Warren. Zondervan: 2002.

"The Relationship of Accountability and Interdependent Behavior to Enhancing Team Consequences" by Patricia M. Fandt. *Group & Organization Studies,* 16(3). Sage Publications, Inc.: 1991.

The 7 Habits of Highly Effective People: Powerful Lessons in Personal Change by Stephen R. Covey. Simon & Schuster, Inc.: 1989.

The 10 Natural Laws of Successful Time and Life Management by Hyrum W. Smith. Warner Books, Inc.: 1994.

The Trust Factor by Robert T. Whipple. Leadergrow, Inc.: 2003.

The 21 Irrefutable Laws of Leadership by John Maxwell & Zig Zigler. Nelson Business: 1998.

"Towards a Process Model of Individual Change in Organizations" by Jennifer M. George & Gareth R. Jones. *Human Relations,* 54(4). Sage Publications Ltd.: 2001.

"Validating Generational Differences: A Legitimate Diversity and Leadership Issue" by Paul M. Arsensult. *Leadership & Organization Development Journal,* 25(1/2). Emerald Group Publishing Limited: 2004.

What Queen Esther Knew by Connie Glaser & Barbara Smalley. Rodale: 2003.

Who Moved My Cheese? by Spencer Johnson, M.D. G. P. Putnam & Sons: 1998.

"Who's Accountable?" by George Gates. *Paper & Pulp,* Miller Freeman Inc.: 2005.

"Why Innovation Happens When Happy People Fight" by Robert I. Sutton. *Ivey Business Journal,* 67(2). Ivey Business Journal: 2002.

"Why People Lie" by Mark Kendall. *The Press-Enterprise,* Press Enterprise: 1998.

Glossary

Accountability—the obligation and willingness of a person to accept responsibility

Appraisal—an evaluation of the significance or value of an individual's performance for an organization over a period of time

Assessment—like appraisal, an assessment determines the importance or value of something

Authenticity—the quality of being fully trustworthy and exactly what is claimed

"Big Picture"—a perspective that considers or understands all elements of a situation or issue

Behaviors—the way a person acts, functions, or reacts

Budgeting—a plan for the coordination of resources and expenditures for a particular purpose

Career Development—how individuals manage their careers within and between organizations; how organizations structure the career progress of their members

Career Objectives—individuals' goals which need to be achieved as part of their career development plan

Character—a person's level of moral excellence and firmness

Coaching—to direct or train others in their job responsibilities and team strategies

Commitment—to agree to or pledge to perform a specific action in the future

Conflict Management—intervention that maximizes the benefits of conflict situations while minimizing the negative consequences

Critical Thinking—a method of thinking by which we question not only the origin and validity of our own opinions and views, but seek and analyze information to guide our beliefs and actions more objectively

Decision Making—the process of defining all of the possible actions which may be taken, as well the strengths and weaknesses of each action, and selecting the action that best addresses the situation

Delegation—the act of giving authority to act for another

Development Path—see Career Development

Direction-Setting Level—positions within the structure of the organization that participate in determining the strategic purpose and resulting actions to be taken on behalf of the company

Employment Law—the laws that govern employment-related issues

Emulate—to imitate

Entry-Level Position—a position within an organization that is performed under close supervision and has no authority over others

Evaluation—a process that determines the worth of something through appraisal or study

Formula—a statement intended to express a principle for action

Goal Setting—the act of determining clear objectives that are shared with every participant to ensure that expectations are understood and success is defined

Habits—behavior patterns acquired by frequent repetition

Innovation—the act of making new or renewing

Interpersonal Skill—a person's ability to interact with others in a manner that helps them achieve desired results

Invention—the creation of something new

Leader—a person who inspires others to do a job better because they are going somewhere others want to go

Leadership Development—the process by which a person works to acquire and enhance the skills needed to influence others and reach organizational objectives

Leadership Effectiveness—the best use of an individual's skills in influencing employees to achieve more than they would have accomplished otherwise

Leadership Progression—the structural path a person within a leadership position has followed to arrive in their current role

Leadership Style—the behaviors associated with the approach and methods used by a leader to obtain organizational results

Level of Authority—the power of an individual to take action on behalf of his or her organization

Mentor—a trusted counselor or guide

Milestone—a significant point in development

Mission Statement—a description of the unique attributes that define how an organization's purpose will be achieved

Motivation—the stimulus that causes a person to act

Organization—the result of steps taken by a group of individuals to form a coherent unity or functioning whole

Organizational Units—subsets of an organization that have been formed to accomplish predefined objectives

Paradigm—a state of work progression in which procedures, expectations, and organizational attitudes have become fixed and adverse to change

Performance Management—a defined and formalized process of assessing employee contributions that establishes personal goals which need to be achieved within an established period of time in order to contribute to organizational and personal success

Proficiency—having advanced knowledge or skill

Project Planning—the process by which a detailed estimate of the resources, schedule, detailed steps, and costs are determined to accomplish a predetermined change initiative

Promotion—advancement in position or rank

Real—genuine; not artificial or fraudulent in any way

Role Model—a person whose behaviors, attitudes, and performance represent what is expected of others

Routines—fixed actions that follow a regular course

Strategic Planning—the method used by an organization to establish objectives and the tactics necessary to achieve them

Structure—the arrangement of power in an organizational body

Team Building—a process or method by which group performance is improved through utilization of individual skills, collaboration, and unification

Time Management—methods or techniques employed to maximize productivity and efficiency in time use

Timeline—a schedule of events and significant achievements

Traditions—beliefs, customs, or knowledge handed down from one person to another

Vision Statement—a statement of an organization's ultimate purpose

Index